MICROWAVE
BAKING

MICROWAVE
BAKING

Val Collins

DAVID & CHARLES
Newton Abbot   London   North Pomfret (Vt)

With grateful thanks to my husband, family and friends for their patience, encouragement and guidance.

British Library Cataloguing in Publication Data
Collins, Val
   Microwave baking.
   1. Microwave Cookery
   2. Baking
   I. Title
   641.7'1   TX832

ISBN 0-7153-8018-4
Library of Congress Catalog Card Number 80-67395

Printed in The Netherlands
by Smeets Offset BV, Weert
for David & Charles (Publishers) Limited
Brunel House Newton Abbot Devon

Published in the United States of America
by David & Charles Inc
North Pomfret Vermont 05053 USA

Contents

Introduction

For me, the delights of microwave baking are the near-instant results which may be achieved and the joy of watching a cake or pudding mixture rise up and cook as if by magic, knowing of the savings in time and energy over cooking by traditional methods. Baking by microwave dispels the idea that home baking has almost gone out of fashion in these days of convenience foods when a range of commercial products in the shops are ready to tempt you to buy.

Most people have fond memories of coming home from school or the office to a kitchen where the delicious smells of home baking still linger and a range of freshly baked bread and cakes are awaiting admiration and instant sampling. For the cook, too, there is much to be said for the satisfaction and pride which is felt in creating so many mouthwatering goodies, when the family come home eager to taste. No commercially produced cake can ever taste like the home-baked one, made with fresh eggs and butter.

But as new technology in the form of electric mixers has taken the arm-ache out of beating and whisking, so now the microwave cooker can bring home baking back into this world of convenience foods. Freshly baked bread, cakes and puddings can be produced from the microwave, often cooked in less time than they took to prepare. Whilst a cake can be prepared and cooked at a moment's notice for those unexpected visitors or guests, the microwave cooker also means a cool and steam-free kitchen on baking days when a variety of mixtures can be cooked one after the other. Slaving over a hot stove is a thing of the past!

With no oven to preheat and a saving of up to 70 per cent on normal cooking times, depending on how much you cook, a microwave can cut your cooking fuel bill by as much as half, which means economical baking. Surely all these advantages are just rewards and more than compensate for the absence of traditional browning on cakes with light textures and excellent flavours. A little planning and careful thought to finishing and decorating a microwave-cooked cake, whether it is just dusted with icing sugar or piped heavily with cream, will ensure a worthwhile result, virtually indistinguishable from one which has been baked in a conventional oven.

One might think that with all these advantages a conventional oven is not really necessary. However, the microwave user knows that there are a few baked products which just cannot be cooked satisfactorily in the microwave – Yorkshire puddings, pancakes, meringues and some pastry for example. This is when the microwave cooker as an aid to baking makes an ideal partner to the conventional oven. Fillings and sauces can be prepared and cooked in the microwave whilst flan cases and pancakes are being cooked conventionally. Bread dough can be proved and part baked in the microwave and, if a crisp crust is preferred, finished off in the conventional oven. By combining these two methods of cooking, you are getting the best of both worlds and you will find reference to this throughout the book where applicable.

For the microwave users who have already taken their first steps into the world of microwave cookery, this book is intended to help develop their culinary skills in the art of baking by microwave.

Useful information

The quantities for recipes in this book are given in metric and imperial measurements; in the following tables, American measurements are also given for comparison. Exact conversions do not always give acceptable working quantities and so the metric equivalents are rounded off into units of 25 grams. This may mean that the overall volume of the cooked product varies very slightly, but from experience I have found that this has little effect on the final result.

Measurement of ingredients

	Metric	*Imperial*
Weight	25 grams	1 ounce
	50g	2oz
Weigh and measure as	75g	3oz
accurately as possible and	100g	4oz
do not mix metric and	150g	5oz
imperial weights in one	175g	6oz
recipe as all measurements	200g	7oz
are proportionate.	225g	8oz
Imperial and American	250g	9oz
measurements in weight	275g	10oz
and length are the same	300g	11oz
	350g	12oz
	375g	13oz
	400g	14oz
	425g	15oz
	450g	16oz (1lb)
	475g	17oz
	500g ($\frac{1}{2}$kg)	18oz
	550g	19oz
	575g	20oz (1$\frac{1}{4}$lb)
Length	1.25 centimetres	$\frac{1}{2}$ inch
	2.5cm	1in
	15.0cm	6in
	17.5cm	7in
	20.0cm	8in
	22.5cm	9in
	25.0cm	10in

	Metric	*Imperial*	*American*
Liquid	150 millilitres	$\frac{1}{4}$ pint	$\frac{2}{3}$ cup
Measurements in liquid	275ml	$\frac{1}{2}$pt	1$\frac{1}{4}$ cups
and volume are different	425ml	$\frac{3}{4}$pt	2 cups
and these charts show the	550ml	1pt	2$\frac{1}{2}$ cups
equivalents using the	850ml	1$\frac{1}{2}$pt	3$\frac{3}{4}$ cups
American 8 ounce	1000ml (1 litre)	1$\frac{3}{4}$pt	4$\frac{1}{2}$ cups
measuring cup	1150ml	2pt	5 cups

Volume

butter	225g	$\frac{1}{2}$lb	1 cup
sugar	225g	$\frac{1}{2}$lb	1 cup
flour	225g	$\frac{1}{2}$lb	2 cups
icing sugar	225g	$\frac{1}{2}$lb	$1\frac{1}{2}$ cups
rice	225g	$\frac{1}{2}$lb	1 cup
dried fruits	225g	$\frac{1}{2}$lb	$1\frac{1}{2}$ cups
breadcrumbs	225g	$\frac{1}{2}$lb	4 cups
grated cheese	225g	$\frac{1}{2}$lb	2 cups

Spoon measures

All spoon measures used	5ml teaspoon	1 tsp	1 tsp
in recipes throughout the	15ml tablespoon	1 tbsp	1 tbsp
book are level unless	$1\frac{1}{2} \times$ 15ml tbsp	$1\frac{1}{2}$ tbsp	2 tbsp
otherwise stated and are	$2 \times$ 15ml tbsp	2 tbsp	3 tbsp
best used only for small	(or 30ml)		
quantities	$4 \times$ 15ml tbsp	4 tbsp	5 tbsp
	(or 60ml)		

Terminology

Imperial	American
double cream	heavy cream
single cream	light cream
soured cream	sour cream
demerara sugar	brown sugar
icing sugar	confectioners sugar
black treacle	dark molasses
golden syrup	light corn syrup
clear honey	thin honey
condensed milk	full cream sweetened milk
wholemeal flour	wholewheat flour
plain flour	all-purpose flour
self-raising flour	all-purpose flour with double acting baking powder
minced beef	ground beef
grade 4 eggs	medium eggs
plain chocolate	bitter chocolate
vanilla essence	vanilla extract
cornflour	cornstarch
digestive biscuits	graham crackers
girdle scones	griddle scones
clingfilm	saran wrap
greaseproof paper	wax paper
kitchen paper	paper towels

Conventional oven temperature chart

Oven temperatures		°C	°F	Gas
VERY COOL		110	225	$\frac{1}{4}$
		130	250	$\frac{1}{2}$
COOL		140	275	1
		150	300	2
MODERATE		160	325	3
		180	350	4
MODERATE/HOT		190	375	5
		200	400	6
HOT		220	425	7
		230	450	8
VERY HOT		240	475	9

For those microwave users who wish to combine microwave and conventional cooking, this chart gives the comparative temperatures and settings between electric and gas ovens

The microwave cooker

Microwave cookers have been known in the catering industry for many years and since the first domestic model was launched in America in the mid 1950s new developments have now made a very wide choice of models available.

Standard units with basic on/off controls are gradually being introduced with additional features such as defrost controls, variable power or selector controls, turntables, browning elements and temperature probes. There are now available some models with sophisticated electronic touch control systems. With no knobs, dials or switches, the cooker is operated simply by touching the appropriate section of the control panel.

The design of all these features varies between the models but they are all similar in appearance and the basic principle of microwave cooking is the same. Before beginning to use the microwave cooker, it is important to know how it operates and to read and understand all the facts given in the manufacturer's instructions. This information, together perhaps with a reputable book on basic microwave cooking, will provide explicit detail about the behaviour of microwave energy and on the operation and care of the appliance.

The microwave cooker controls consist mainly of one or two timers, a start or cook button with indicator light and a master switch. Of these features, the timer is important as microwave cooking is gauged by time, not time and temperature. With the introduction of the variable power or selector control there is a greater flexibility and control of the cooking speed which may be compared with the equivalent of conventional oven settings. With many food items this is unnecessary but it can be invaluable for those foods or dishes which may benefit from a longer, slower cooking period.

There are two methods used by manufacturers to vary the power input into the oven. Either the microwave energy is cycled on and off at varying rates depending on the setting chosen, or the power input into the oven is altered to provide continuous but lower speed cooking.

Different manufacturers portray the description of the variable power settings on the control panels of their models in different ways. It is useful to compare these in chart form to enable you to adapt the cooking times given in this book to suit your particular model.

Variable power settings and time chart

Descriptions of settings	1 KEEP WARM LOW	2 SIMMER MEDIUM/LOW	3 STEW	4 DEFROST MEDIUM	5 BAKE MEDIUM/HIGH	6 ROAST	7 FULL/HIGH NORMAL
Approximate % input	25%	30%	40%	50%	60%	75%	100%
Approximate power input (watts)	150W	200W	250W	300W	400W	500W	650W
Cooking time (minutes)							
1	4	$3\frac{1}{4}$	$2\frac{1}{2}$	2	$1\frac{3}{4}$	$1\frac{1}{4}$	1
2	8	$6\frac{3}{4}$	5	4	$3\frac{1}{4}$	$2\frac{3}{4}$	2
3	12	10	$7\frac{1}{2}$	6	5	4	3
4	16	$13\frac{1}{4}$	10	8	$6\frac{3}{4}$	$5\frac{1}{4}$	4
5	20	$16\frac{3}{4}$	$12\frac{1}{2}$	10	$8\frac{1}{4}$	$6\frac{3}{4}$	5
6	24	20	15	12	10	8	6
7	28	$23\frac{1}{4}$	$17\frac{1}{2}$	14	$11\frac{1}{4}$	$9\frac{1}{4}$	7
8	32	$26\frac{3}{4}$	20	16	$13\frac{1}{4}$	$10\frac{3}{4}$	8
9	36	30	$22\frac{1}{2}$	18	15	12	9
10	40	$33\frac{1}{4}$	25	20	$16\frac{1}{2}$	$13\frac{1}{4}$	10

For times greater than 10 min simply add the figures in the appropriate columns	These figures are intended as a guide only as much depends on the temperature, density and thickness of the food and the shape and size of the cooking container

Microwave users with models which have one variable setting only (this may be marked defrost or medium) can also use the time chart as a guide on this lower setting. Advice on cooking times is given in each recipe and all cooking is carried out on 'normal', 'full' or 'high' settings unless otherwise stated. Just as conventional ovens vary in temperatures at recommended settings so microwave ovens vary in their speed of cooking. Recipes in this book were tested in a model with a power input into the oven capacity of 650 watts. The wattage of your own cooker may be higher or lower than this, in which case the cooking time must be decreased for the higher-rated models and increased for the lower-rated ones. In addition to this, cooking times can vary slightly between models with the same rated input. Therefore, try out a few of the recipes and compare the actual cooking times with the recommended cooking times and remember to adjust accordingly for the other recipes throughout the book.

Microwave baking techniques

Although it may be a popularly held belief that microwave cookers cannot bake, just watching a cake mixture rise in the microwave will convince you that it can! The result is inevitably most successful with a light texture and good flavour. But be prepared to open the oven door to have a closer look at the food to see how it is cooking just as if you were using a conventional oven. Most food is very good tempered and will easily survive the short time the door is open. In fact, heat is produced within the food so quickly again after the microwave is restarted that little or no harm will occur to even a light sponge cake.

Always underbake rather than overbake by giving the food slightly less time than recommended. It is better to put the dish back into the oven for another minute or two if not quite done rather than end up with dried-out food which cannot be rectified.

Bread, cakes, pastry and puddings cooked in the microwave do not have that golden brown appearance associated generally with baked products from a conventional oven. In most cases this really does not matter at all or can be overcome by decorating or garnishing with a supply of icings, frostings, nuts, seeds, herbs and spices ready to hand. Alternatively, food can be finished in a hot conventional oven or placed under the grill for a few minutes to brown the top.

Do not think that baking by microwave means that you must learn completely new cooking techniques. In fact, most of the basic rules still apply. It is just a case of bending and adapting those rules and yourself to this new method of baking. Special points to watch for are mentioned in the various recipe sections but below are a few reminders of the factors which govern successful results.

Texture

As microwave cooking is so fast, differences in texture will show up more quickly in the end result. A lighter mixture allows the microwave energy to penetrate more easily than a heavier one and will cook faster.

Moisture

Moisture too can affect cooking times as microwave energy reacts mainly on water molecules. Some of the recipes in this book have been adjusted to use more liquid than you are perhaps used to in order to ensure a good even rise and moist result, particularly in cake mixtures.

Starting temperature

Differences in the temperature of the food when placed into the microwave will affect the length of cooking time required. The colder the food, the longer it will take to cook, so allowances must be made when using food straight from the refrigerator or freezer.

Quantity

As the quantity of food placed into the cooker is increased, so the cooking time must be lengthened accordingly. As a guide, when doubling the food to be cooked allow between $\frac{1}{3}$ and $\frac{1}{2}$ extra cooking time. Similarly, if you halve the quantities for the recipes given in this book, initially give $\frac{2}{3}$ of the cooking time, allowing up to $\frac{3}{4}$ if necessary. For example:
   If single recipe quantity requires 12 min
   Double recipe quantity would require 16–18 min
   Half recipe quantity would require 8–9 min

Arrangement of the food in the cooker

When heating or cooking a number of rolls, buns or cakes for example, they should be of even size where possible and arranged in a circle on a plate or on the cooking shelf.

Stirring and turning

The stirring of food during a heating or cooking process is recommended in some dishes to ensure an even distribution of heat. When it is not possible to stir, particularly when cooking baked products, then simply rearrange the dish in the oven cavity by giving it a half or quarter turn. This is not always necessary if a microwave cooker with a turntable is available.

Standing time

All foods carry on cooking to a degree when removed from the oven and some food items will require this standing or resting period to assist with the heating or cooking process. A cake or pudding, for example, should be removed from the microwave when the top is still slightly moist and left to stand until cooking is complete. When cooking a flatter dish like a quiche or flan, a standing time may be allowed during the cooking process to allow the heat to penetrate from the sides into the cooler centre.

Covering foods

It is not normally advisable to cover 'baked' products when cooking in the microwave as this would hold in the moisture. If dishes require covering, then this information will be given in specific recipes; for example, 'steamed' puddings are covered with clingfilm to keep in the moisture but the clingfilm should be slit with the pointed end of a knife to allow air to escape.

Utensils

One of the advantages of microwave cooking is that foods may be cooked and served in the same dish. Also owing to the fact that heat is only produced within the food itself, nothing burns on so containers are generally easier to clean and food tends not to stick.

Although the term 'baking' conjures up a range of metal baking trays and patty tins, microwave energy is reflected from metal which means that aluminium, aluminium foil, tin, copper and stainless steel containers must not be used. However, microwave energy passes through glass, pottery and china and so, provided they have no metal trim, makes them all excellent containers when baking in the microwave.

Some pottery and china absorb more microwave energy which makes them less efficient. If in doubt, it is worth checking a container by carrying out a simple test. Place the dish into the microwave together with a glass of water. After $1\frac{1}{2}$ minutes cooking time the water should be hot and the dish cool. If the reverse is found then the dish must not be used. On the other hand, if the dish and the water are both warm, then the dish could be used, but as it is absorbing some microwave energy it is less efficient and cooking times would be longer. Most dishes remain cool as microwave energy passes through them to be absorbed by the food, but during cooking there may be some heat transfer from the food to the dish so be careful when removing them from the cooker.

Suitable containers

To the new microwave user, I normally recommend sorting through the containers and dishes already available before embarking on buying new ones. Quite often it is possible to improvise. For example, placing a glass tumbler in the centre of a round dish makes a mould for a ring cake; glass, pottery or china soufflé dishes make ideal containers for bread and cake mixtures; clay or plastic flower pots can be used for baking an unusual-shaped loaf; small cakes can be cooked in paper cases placed inside cups and very often the microwave cooker shelf makes an ideal baking tray. Ovenproof glass and pottery plates and flan dishes can be used equally well in the conventional oven or microwave cooker for tarts and quiches and most cupboards have an assortment of glass or pottery bowls, casseroles and pie dishes for puddings, crumbles and pies.

Suitable microwave baking containers

Shapes and sizes

Generally the more regular the shape of the container the better it is for even heating or cooking. A round dish is preferable to an oval one and a straight-sided dish better than one which is curved. A container which is slightly rounded at the corners rather than one with square corners will help to prevent food from overcooking at these sharper edges. Larger, shallow dishes are preferable to smaller, deep ones as the greater surface area allows more penetration of the microwave energy.

It is important to ensure that the container is large enough to hold the food to be heated or cooked. Cake mixtures in particular rise extremely well to almost double their volume, so remember to only fill the container half full of the uncooked mixture. Different manufacturers of oven glassware and pottery dishes may quote the size of the dish by giving either the base or top measurement. When the untensil is straight sided, of course this does not matter at all, but when the dish is tapered at the sides, it can make a difference to the overall volume. Where I have quoted a dish size in the recipes, it is the base measurement of the container which is given.

Special microwave containers

There is now a wider choice of special microwave cooking containers and dishes available on the market, but the selection depends on your needs and requirements. A muffin dish, for example, apart from its obvious use, could make an ideal shape for individual cakes and a microwave baking tray would be useful. Some of these utensils are intended for conventional cooking as well as microwave cooking and other types are suitable for both microwave and the freezer, which are added advantages.

Browning dishes

These are specially designed for use in the microwave cooker. In appearance they are normal glass ceramic or pyroflam dishes but have a special tin oxide coating on the base. When the dish is preheated in the microwave cooker, the base absorbs microwave energy and gets very hot. Food such as steak, chicken portions, sausages, bacon or chops are placed onto the hot base which sears the outside of the food, similar to grilling or frying, whilst microwave energy cooks the food.

They are not normally suitable for browning baked products during a cooking process, for example when cooking a cake or a loaf of bread, but I have described their use in some recipes which require a light 'frying' application such as breadslices and girdle scones. When cooking a second batch in the browning dish, any food residue which may have stuck to the base of the dish during the first cook must be scraped or cleared before beginning the second. Usually the browning dish will require a further 2–3 minutes preheating time to boost the temperature of the base before cooking the second batch of food.

Linings

The use of clingfilm to line dishes has the advantage of enabling delicate cakes and puddings to be removed more easily from the container (especially when still warm) and placed the right way up on the cooling rack. Also it practically eliminates the need to wash the dish afterwards. The one disadvantage of using clingfilm as a lining is that it is sometimes difficult to obtain neat corners and edges which may be important to the shape of the cooked result. In this case, it is preferable to line the base of the greased dish with greaseproof paper. It is better not to dust with flour as this is inclined to result in a doughy crust forming on the outside of the baked product.

Paper

Kitchen paper may be used in the microwave to absorb moisture when reheating or cooking pastry items. Either the food can be placed on a layer of kitchen paper or alternatively a piece may be placed lightly over the top of the dish during the heating period. When baking a pastry flan case blind, kitchen paper is used instead of greaseproof paper to absorb the moisture from the pastry during cooking.

Baked products, either in complete dishes or individual portions, may be placed on paper plates, doyleys or serviettes for reheating prior to serving. Do not use coloured or patterned paper as the colour may tend to transfer on to the food.

Wicker and straw baskets

These may be used in the microwave for short-term heating only as long exposure to microwave energy may cause them to dry out and crack. However, they are absolutely ideal when thawing or reheating bread or rolls before a meal or dinner party.

Aluminium foil

If you notice during a cooking or heating process that part of the food is overcooking, perhaps at an outside edge, then it is possible to mask this part of the food from the microwave energy with a small, smooth piece of aluminium foil. However the foil must not be allowed to touch the interior sides or back of the oven cavity and it is advisable to check with the manufacturer's instructions with reference to the use of aluminium foil in your particular model.

In and out of the freezer

People use freezers in different ways. Some fill their freezers with joints and cuts of meat, fruit and vegetables and enjoy cooking from scratch when meals are required. Others prefer to stock up with a range of commercially frozen products. Personally I find that I tend to keep a variety of these foods but must say that my own precooked and frozen foods take pride of place. In this way I have a stockpile of meals and snacks ready at a moment's notice and of course the cooking for the freezer can be done when I have the time. The freezer and my microwave cooker go hand in hand and to be without either one of them would be like losing a valuable kitchen helper.

Sometimes I cook or bake single items in the microwave and freeze them ready for a specific occasion, or I may bake a quantity of flan or quiche bases in the conventional oven. I cheat a little here and never add sugar to basic flan pastry so that they are then available for the sweet or savoury filling to be added and cooked by microwave when required. This also works in reverse as it is useful to have fillings for pies prepared by microwave and frozen ready to be placed in a pie dish, covered with pastry and cooked conventionally.

Taking precooked, baked products from the freezer to thaw by microwave requires some special attention as overheating could spell disaster, resulting in an inedible hard mass and leaving you with a feeling of wasted money, time and effort.

Most small items can be thawed on normal or high setting in a matter of seconds. Larger loaves, pies and puddings will require standing periods to ensure an even transfer of heat into the centre. Alternatively a covered bowl of water placed into the oven cavity when defrosting larger items will absorb some of the microwave energy, thereby slowing down the thawing process for more even results. To a degree, standing times can be almost eliminated in microwave cookers with the facility of a defrost or variable power control. In any case, whichever method you prefer, the same basic rule still applies – as soon as the food feels warm to touch on the outside edges, leave it to rest or heat equalise at room temperature, in or out of the oven cavity as convenient. If then it is not fully thawed just give it another minute or two of microwave energy.

The advice and information given below does not alway refer to recipes in this book. For example sausage rolls cannot be successfully baked in the microwave but you can thaw frozen ones, remembering to place a piece of kitchen paper into the microwave to absorb moisture. A trick I have learned, having thawed a pastry dish in the microwave, is to place it in the conventional oven or under a grill with the plates to warm – even just a few minutes will help to crispen the pastry prior to serving although some pastry will crispen slightly during its standing time.

Most baked products can be frozen successfully and therefore I have only noted those recipes in the book which require special freezing attention.

Thawing individual foods

Most baked products can be thawed uncovered on their serving plate or dish. Sliced bread or rolls may be placed in a cotton, linen or paper serviette inside a wicker or straw basket. Cakes can be put on to doyleys, remembering that a number of small cakes, buns, scones, etc, are better arranged in a circle to ensure even thawing. Biscuits and pastry items are usually better for being thawed on kitchen paper to absorb moisture before being transferred to their serving dish or plate.

Biscuits

Most biscuits will thaw out very quickly at room temperature; one or two should be heated in the microwave for no longer than 10–15 seconds and a plate of biscuits for no longer than 1 minute. Then leave them to stand for a few minutes before serving.

Breads

Remember that the texture of the bread will affect thawing times. Light Vienna or French bread will thaw more quickly than the heavier steam-baked variety. Depending on this, one roll or slice of bread may be thawed in 10–25 seconds, two would take 15–30 seconds and three 20–35 seconds. A thick slice from a large prepacked sliced loaf will take approximately 30 seconds to thaw.

Crumpets and slices of bread to be toasted in a toaster or under a grill do not need to be thawed as they can be toasted from the frozen state. Muffins, teacakes, buns and scones may be thawed for 10–20 seconds in the microwave before being cut and toasted, otherwise leave them to stand for 2 minutes before serving.

Small loaves of bread should be given 1 minute of microwave energy followed by 1 minute standing, repeated until thawed. For large loaves, these times can be increased to 2 minutes.

Cakes

A small individual cake or slice of cake takes approximately 15–30 seconds and then should be left to stand for 2 minutes. Several small cakes to be thawed should be heated for no longer than 1 minute before testing and, if one feels warm to the touch, it should be removed from the oven.

A cake of 17.5–20cm (7–8in) diameter will require only 2–3 minutes in the microwave before leaving it to stand for 5–10 minutes. It is preferable not to defrost by microwave those light gâteaux and cakes which have been filled or decorated with fresh cream, butter cream or chocolate; as the cream may melt before the cake is thawed, allow to defrost naturally. However, if your microwave cooker has a variable power facility it is possible to commence the thawing process by using the lowest setting possible for just 1 or 2 minutes.

Flans

Flans, quiches, tarts and plate pies of 17.5–20cm (7–8in) diameter, depending on their fillings, require a 2–4 minute heating time followed by a 2–4 minute standing period repeated until thawed. Alternatively heat on a defrost setting for 5–6 minutes. If it is not quite thawed, either leave it to stand at room temperature or place it back into the cooker for another minute or two.

Baked or unbaked flan cases frozen separately do not normally require thawing before filling and cooking in the microwave, although a little extra cooking time should be allowed.

Individual portions do not need more than about 1 minute to heat through once thawed.

Pancakes

Pancakes which have been cooked conventionally and then frozen can be thawed and reheated most successfully in the microwave. Pancakes which have been frozen without fillings, layered with greaseproof or kitchen paper, need to be heated just for a few seconds until they can be separated when they will thaw out quite quickly at room temperature.

Frozen, filled pancakes should be placed on a plate or in a dish and covered with clingfilm. Four will need 2–3 minutes heating followed by 2–3 minutes standing, repeated until the filling is thawed. Alternatively heat on a defrost setting for approximately 5 minutes, allowing an extra minute or two if required. When the filling is completely thawed, reheat on full or normal setting for $1\frac{1}{2}$–2 minutes until hot through.

Pies

The difficulty in thawing larger cooked pies is in getting the filling thawed before the pastry or topping is overheated. However this can be done successfully by masking the pie topping with aluminium foil so that the pie filling is being heated from the base only. Alternatively, heat the dish until the pastry is warm to the touch and then allow to thaw naturally at room temperature.

It is often preferable, rather than heating the complete pie to cut it into individual portions and heat each one separately for 1–2 minutes on its serving plate. Alternatively, the entire dish may be heated by repeated short heating periods followed by standing periods, until hot. If your microwave has a defrost control, heat through using this setting when standing periods are not usually required.

Puddings

Most puddings can be thawed and reheated in one operation. Allow 2–3 minutes heating time followed by 1–2 minutes standing time before serving. Individual portions should be heated for approximately 1 minute each.

For suet crust puddings with meat or fruit fillings, follow the information for pies given above. Although it is possible to freeze suet crust pastry dishes, they are at their best when freshly cooked.

Pizzas

Pizzas can be thawed and reheated in 3–5 minutes depending on size. Individual portions cut from a larger pizza may be reheated in 1–1½ minutes.

Sausage rolls

One sausage roll should be placed on kitchen paper to absorb moisture and heated for 15–30 seconds to thaw and left to rest for 1 minute before serving; if required hot, return to the microwave for 15 seconds to heat through. 4 sausage rolls will take about 1–1½ minutes to thaw and heat through depending on their size.

Important points to remember

* All the theory regarding ingredients and mixing methods applied to preparing food for baking are the same whether cooking conventionally or by microwave. It is only the quantities of those ingredients which may alter.

* The basic techniques used for general cooking in the microwave still apply when baking by microwave.

* All cooking is carried out in the microwave cooker using normal setting 7, high or full power unless otherwise stated.

* The recommended cooking times are intended as a guide only as so much depends on the power input to the microwave oven cavity, the shape, material and size of the dish, the temperature of the food at the commencement of cooking and the depth of food in the dish.

* If the quantities of food placed in the cooker are increased or decreased, then the cooking times must be adjusted accordingly.

* Always undercook rather than overcook the food by cooking for a little less time than the recipe recommends, allowing the extra time if required.

* Microwave cooking does not brown baked food in the traditional way but dishes can be finished off in a conventional oven or under a grill if you feel it is necessary.

* Metal baking tins or metal trimmed dishes must not be used in the microwave cooker.

* If the cooked or reheated food has become generally hard or dry, then overcooking or insufficient liquid content is indicated; remember to cook for a shorter period next time and check that the liquid measurements were correct.

* If the cooked food is hard or dry in patches, it could mean that either the ingredients were not mixed together properly or that the dish was not turned sufficiently during cooking.

* Some microwave cooking instructions are given for models with variable power control settings, but it is still possible to cook the dish on models without this facility by referring to the 'Variable Power Settings and Time Chart' on page 11 and calculating the time required for cooking on full, normal or high power. The automatic intermittent 'off' periods can be achieved manually by allowing the dish to rest at 1–2 minute intervals throughout the cooking duration.

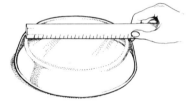

* Any warming or heating of food during the preparation of a dish is carried out in the microwave cooker and this information is given for each recipe in the method. In this way, you are using the microwave as a tool – to work for you in the kitchen. However, I have included, where appropriate, the alternative method of conventional baking and the utensil required for those of you who may prefer traditional browning. Where I have suggested that a container is lined with clingfilm, this is for microwave cooking only. *Do not* line baking tins or dishes with clingfilm when cooking conventionally as it will melt; use lightly greased, greaseproof paper instead.

* Where the size of the dish is quoted in the recipes, it is the base measurement of the container which is given.

Breads

There are not many people who can pass a baker's kitchen without delighting in the delicious aroma of freshly made bread. Yet one of the things that detracts from making your own is the time required for proving the dough when normally a warm place (like the airing cupboard) must be found for the long, slow, rising process; when bread-making, patience is a virtue! But with a microwave cooker, the dough for a ½kg (1lb) loaf can be proved in less than half the normal time by giving it combinations of short bursts of energy for 15 seconds and standing times of 5–10 minutes which allow an even distribution of warmth through the dough, ensuring a steady rise.

This fast, trouble-free method is a great benefit to the busy housewife, but successful bread-making depends on more than just proving the dough; you should understand the ingredients and know how to use them.

Yeast

Yeast is a living bacteria which leavens the dough and gives bread its characteristic flavour. Yeast requires warm, moist conditions in which to grow and is affected by extremes of heat and cold.

High temperatures will kill the yeast and stop its growth, for example during the baking process. But this can also happen during the mixing if the liquid added is too hot, or during the proving if it is subjected to too much heat when the dough may begin to cook around the edges. Low temperatures do not kill the dough but simply retard its growth and therefore the mixed dough can be stored in the refrigerator for a short period or in the freezer for a longer time.

Dried yeast is available in granular form and is used in the recipes in this book as it is usually more easily available. The instructions for using dried yeast are given on the packet or tin but normally it is left to soak and activate in some of the liquid from the recipe, with a little sugar added, for about 8–12 minutes. During this time, the other ingredients can be weighed and measured.

Fresh yeast is available in compacted blocks; it is usually less easy to obtain but can sometimes be bought from a local bakery. If you wish to use fresh yeast, you must double the amount given in the recipe for dried yeast and add 1 × 5ml tsp sugar (1tsp) to bring it to a liquid. Fresh yeast can be stored in the refrigerator for up to two weeks or even longer in the freezer.

Flour

A special bread flour can be used for white bread and is known as 'strong' flour. It has a high gluten content and will mix to a greater volume and give a lighter texture than all-purpose flours. However, strong flour can be difficult to obtain and plain flour may be used. Flours vary in their ability to absorb moisture so it is difficult to give the exact quantities of liquid – always be prepared to add a drop more if the mixture feels dry.

Salt

Salt adds flavour to the bread and is usually added to the flour or dissolved in the liquid ingredient in the recipe.

Milk, eggs and butter

These give flavour, richness, colour and texture to the basic dough mixture and extend the keeping qualities of the bread.

Kneading, shaping and baking

When kneading the dough, the mixture is placed on a lightly floured, smooth surface. With your fingers, pull the edge of the dough over to the centre and push out again with the heel of your hand. Gradually you will develop a rhythmic movement with both hands, creating a circular motion around the edge of the dough. Alternatively, mixing and kneading can be carried out using the dough hook of an electric mixer.

Kneading the dough mixture develops the gluten in the flour and helps to stretch it evenly. When the dough becomes smooth and leaves the sides of the bowl, it has had sufficient kneading. Richer mixtures with the addition of milk, eggs or butter are usually wetter and resemble a heavy batter. These very soft doughs are ready when the mixture is smooth with many tiny air bubbles visible just under the surface.

After kneading, the dough is then placed in a bowl, covered with clingfilm and proved until double its size in the microwave cooker as described earlier. If you wish to prove the dough conventionally it should be lightly greased to prevent a skin forming and covered with a damp cloth. This creates a steamy atmosphere, helping the dough to rise. The temperature should be 21–27°C (70–80°F) and the proving process will take about 1 hour.

When the dough has risen sufficiently, it is 'knocked back' or kneaded again to distribute the air bubbles evenly through the dough. Most breads are then shaped and put into their containers or on a baking tray and given a second rising until double their size. This normally takes 15–20 minutes and if proved conventionally can be left in a slightly warmer temperature than the original rising.

When the dough is ready, it should spring back when lightly touched with the fingertips. It is then ready for baking in the microwave cooker or in a hot, preheated conventional oven.

Note: *If the shaped bread dough is to be baked conventionally in a loaf tin or other metal container, on no account must it be proved for the second time in the microwave, but must be allowed to rise naturally in a warm place.*

Scones

Scones are very quickly cooked and can almost be made whilst the rest of the tea is being prepared. They are very popular whether served hot or cold, sweet or savoury and then split and served with butter. Sweet mixtures can be made into a scone round and, when cooked, decorated with glacé icing, nuts and cherries, or may be served with cream and jam. Savoury ones may be sprinkled with cheese and, before serving, quickly reheated in the microwave or toasted under the grill.

For the best results make scones with plain flour and a raising agent which can be baking powder or bicarbonate of soda and cream of tartar. The liquid ingredient is fresh or soured milk.

However, satisfactory results can be obtained using self-raising flour and similar mixtures are used for teabreads and pizza bases made without yeast.

In some parts of Britain, girdle scones are more popular and are traditionally cooked slowly on a lightly greased girdle but, if not available, a thick frying pan makes an ideal substitute. In the microwave cooker, girdle scones can be made by cooking them in a browning dish.

As bicarbonate of soda is a very fast raising agent, soda breads and scone doughs must be handled lightly and mixed quickly using sufficient liquid to make a soft dough. They are then lightly patted or rolled into a round 1.25cm ($\frac{1}{2}$in) thick and cut into triangles, or cut into small rounds with a 5–6.25cm (2–2$\frac{1}{2}$in) cutter. There should be as little delay as possible between mixing and baking and they should be cooked quickly.

If scones are to be cooked on a girdle, they should be rolled thinner and cooked more slowly, otherwise the outside will be overbrowned before the middle is cooked through. This problem is overcome when cooking girdle scones in the browning dish in a microwave cooker as, whilst the outside of the scone is being browned on the base of the dish, microwave energy is cooking the remainder of the dough.

Continental yeast mixtures

Included in this section are coffee breads, usually made from the richer yeast mixtures and so called because they are often served on the continent with coffee, although they may also appear at breakfast and are also suitable for teatime! They should be eaten freshly baked, with or without butter, and are ideal for those who prefer 'not-so-sweet' cakes or buns.

Bread and rolls

White bread (*makes 1 loaf*)
POWER SETTING 7 (FULL OR HIGH)

This is a basic white bread dough which can also be used for pizzas or white rolls

1 × 5ml tsp (1tsp) sugar
275ml ($\frac{1}{2}$pt) water
1 × 5ml tsp (1tsp) dried yeast
450g (1lb) plain flour
1 × 5ml tsp (1tsp) salt
40g (1$\frac{1}{2}$oz) butter or margarine
poppy seeds or sesame seeds
for sprinkling

1 Lightly grease a 15cm (6in) soufflé dish or 900g (2lb) loaf dish and line the base with greaseproof paper.
2 Add the sugar to half the water and warm for 30 sec. Stir in the yeast and leave for 8–12 min to activate.
3 Sift the flour and salt into a bowl and warm for 30 sec. Rub in the butter or margarine finely.
4 Warm the rest of the water for 30 sec and add with the yeast to the flour, adding a little extra water if necessary to make a fairly soft dough. Knead thoroughly until the dough is smooth.
5 Place the dough in a bowl covered with clingfilm and prove by heating for 15 sec and leaving to stand for 5–10 min. Repeat this 3–4 times until the dough has doubled in size.
6 Turn the dough onto a lightly floured surface and knead well until smooth. Shape the dough and place into the prepared container and prove as described previously until double in size.
7 Lightly oil the top of the dough and sprinkle with poppy seeds or sesame seeds.
8 Cook for 5 min, turning once if necessary. Leave to stand for 10 min, then turn out and cool on wire rack.

Alternative conventional bake
Place the dough in a greased loaf dish or tin.
If a metal loaf tin is used, the second proving must be carried out conventionally in a warm place. Cook in a preheated oven at 220°C (425°F) Mark 7 for 20–30 min.

450g (1lb) White Bread
Dough (page 23)

poppy seeds or sesame seeds
for sprinkling

White rolls *(makes 16)*
POWER SETTING 7 (FULL OR HIGH)

These are made from the basic white bread dough

1 Follow the instructions for white bread until the end of the first proving at
stage 5.
2 Turn the dough onto a lightly floured surface and knead well until smooth.
3 Divide the dough into 16 pieces, shape the rolls and place in a circle on a
lightly greased microwave baking tray or oven shelf.
4 Heat for 15 sec and leave to stand for 5–10 min. Repeat until rolls have well
risen.
5 Lightly brush the rolls with oil and sprinkle with poppy seeds or sesame
seeds.
6 Cook 8 at a time for 2 min, rearranging the rolls if necessary halfway
through. Leave to cool on wire rack.

Alternative conventional bake
After the second proving on the microwave shelf, place the rolls on a lightly
greased baking tray. Alternatively, prove on a baking tray in a warm place.
Cook in a preheated oven at 220°C (425°F) Mark 7 for 15–20 min. For a more
glossy finish, the rolls may be brushed with beaten egg before baking.

Alternative shapes for rolls
Plait: Divide dough into three, shape each piece into a long roll and plait
together securing ends firmly.
Twist: Divide dough into two, shape each piece into a long roll and twist
together, securing ends firmly.
Knot: Shape dough into a long roll and tie into a knot.
Rings: Shape dough into a long roll and bend it round to form a ring,
dampen the ends and secure by moulding them together.

Prove and bake as described in the recipe.

450g (1lb) White Bread
Dough (page 23)

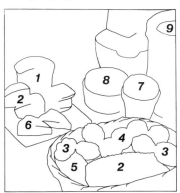

Selection of breads and rolls
1 Dark Rye Bread   2 Light
Wholemeal Bread   3 White
Rolls   4 Light Wholemeal
Rolls   5 Baps   6 Oatmeal Bread
7 Cheese Bread   8 Milk Bread
9 Granary Bread

Baps *(makes 6)*
POWER SETTING 7 (FULL OR HIGH)

*These are light rolls suitable as hamburger buns and make good alternatives to
bread slices when making sandwiches*

1 Follow the instruction for white bread until the end of the first proving
stage 5.
2 Turn the dough onto a lightly floured surface and knead well until smooth.
3 Divide the dough into 6, knead each piece and roll into an oval shape.
Prove and cook 3 at a time.
4 Place 3 on the floured microwave baking tray or shelf, dust with flour.
Heat for 15 sec and leave to stand for 5–10 min. Repeat until well risen.
5 Cook for 2 min, rearranging baps if necessary halfway through. Leave to
cool on wire rack.
6 Repeat with remaining 3 baps.

Alternative conventional bake
Prove the 6 baps in the microwave then place on lightly floured baking trays.
Alternatively, prove on a baking tray in a warm place. Cook in a preheated
oven at 220°C (425°F) Mark 7 for 5 min, then reduce to 200°C (400°F) Mark 6
for a further 15–20 min. The baps should be pale brown when cooked.

450g (1lb) White Bread
Dough (page 23)

Pitta bread (*makes 4 large or 8 small*)
POWER SETTING 7 (FULL OR HIGH)

These are flat Greek-style loaves, often eaten with kebabs

1 Follow the instruction for white bread until the end of the first proving at
   stage 5.
2 Turn the dough onto a lightly floured surface and knead well until smooth.
3 Divide the dough into 4 or 8. Knead each piece and roll into a flat oval.
4 Sprinkle with flour, dampen the edges and fold each oval in half (top to
   bottom), trimming the edges if necessary.
5 Place 1 large or 2 small on the lightly greased microwave shelf and without
   further proving cook for 3–4 min. Repeat with the remaining loaves.
6 Leave to cool on wire rack.

Alternative conventional bake
Place the loaves on lightly greased baking trays and cook in a preheated oven
at 230°C (450°F) Mark 8 for 20–25 min.

Milk bread (*makes 1 loaf*) and milk rolls (*makes 16*)

This is softer, closer-textured bread. Follow the ingredients, method and
cooking time for White Bread and Rolls, substituting milk or milk and water
for the liquid content.

Alternative conventional bake
These doughs may be brushed with beaten egg before cooking to give a rich,
glazed finish.

Note: *These richer doughs may require a slightly longer proving time.*

Cottage loaf (*makes 1*)

Follow the ingredients and method for White Bread but using less water –
220ml (8fl oz) – to make a firmer dough. When shaping, cut two-thirds of the
dough and knead each piece into a bun shape. Place the larger piece onto the

lightly greased microwave shelf, put the small piece on top and secure by pushing your floured little finger right down the centre to the very base. Prove and cook as for white bread.

Light wholemeal bread (makes 1 loaf) and rolls (makes 16)

Follow the ingredients and method for White Bread and Rolls, substituting 225g (½lb) of wholemeal flour for white flour and using sesame seeds or nibbed wheat instead of poppy seeds for sprinkling.

Note: *Wholemeal flours tend to absorb slightly less liquid than the finer flours which should be taken into account when mixing the dough and the proving times may be slightly longer.*

Wholemeal bread (makes 1 loaf)
POWER SETTING 7 (FULL OR HIGH)

This is a coarser-textured wholemeal loaf

1 Lightly grease a 20cm (8in) flan dish and line base with greaseproof paper.
2 Add the sugar to half the water and warm for 30 sec. Stir in the yeast and leave 8–12 min to activate.
3 Place the flour and salt in a bowl and warm for 30 sec. Rub in the butter or margarine finely. Warm the rest of the liquid for 30 sec.
4 Add the yeast and warmed liquid to the flour. Mix well. This should be a soft dough and the quantity of liquid may vary slightly. Knead thoroughly until the dough is smooth.
5 Place the dough in a bowl covered with clingfilm and prove by heating for 15 sec and leave to stand for 5–10 min. Repeat this 3–4 times until double in size.
6 Turn the dough onto a lightly floured surface and knead well until smooth. Shape the dough and place in the prepared container and prove as described previously until double in size.
7 Lightly oil the top of the dough and sprinkle with nibbed wheat.
8 Cook for 5 min, turning once halfway through if necessary. Leave to stand for 10 min and then turn out onto a wire rack to cool.

Alternative conventional bake
Place the dough in a greased flan dish or sandwich tin. If a metal tin is used, the second proving must be carried out conventionally in a warm place. Cook in a preheated oven at 200°C (400°F) Mark 6 for 35–45 min.

1½ × 5ml tsp (1½tsp) soft brown sugar
275 ml (½pt) milk and water mixed, approximately
1 × 5ml tsp (1tsp) dried yeast
450g (1lb) wholemeal flour
2 × 5ml tsp (2tsp) salt
40g (1½oz) butter or margarine
nibbed wheat for sprinkling

Light granary bread (makes 1 loaf)
POWER SETTING 7 (FULL OR HIGH)

1 Lightly grease a 22cm (9in) round dish or 900g (2lb) microwave loaf dish and line the base with greaseproof paper.
2 Add the sugar to a third of the water and warm for 30 sec. Stir in the yeast and leave for 8–12 min to activate.
3 Mix the flours and salt well and warm for 30 sec. Warm the remaining liquid for 45 sec.
4 Add the yeast, oil and sufficient of the remaining liquid to the flour to form a soft dough. Mix well – very little kneading is required – and form into a ball.

1½ × 5ml tsp (1½tsp) soft brown sugar
425ml (¾pt) water, approximately
1 × 5ml tsp (1tsp) dried yeast
450g (1lb) granary meal
100g (4oz) wheatmeal or strong plain flour
1½ × 5ml tsp (1½tsp) salt
2 × 15ml tbsp (2tbsp) oil
nibbed wheat for sprinkling

5 Place the dough into a bowl covered with clingfilm and prove by heating for 15 sec and leaving to stand for 5–10 min. Repeat this 3–4 times until double in size.

6 Turn the dough onto a lightly floured surface, knead well until smooth. Shape the dough and place in the prepared container and prove as described previously until double in size.

7 Lightly oil the surface of the dough and sprinkle with nibbed wheat. Cut two deep cuts crossways over the top.

8 Cook for 5½–6½ min, turning once if necessary. Leave to stand for 10 min and then turn out onto a wire rack to cool.

Alternative conventional bake
Place the dough in a greased round ovenware dish or loaf tin. If a metal tin is used, the second proving must be carried out conventionally in a warm place. Place dough in an unheated oven, set to 230°C (450°F) Mark 8 for 45 min, reduce to 200°C (400°F) Mark 6 for 20–25 min.

Light rye bread *(makes 1 loaf)*
POWER SETTING 7 (FULL OR HIGH)

1½ × 5ml tsp (1½tsp) brown sugar
425ml (¾pt) water, approximately
1 × 5ml tsp (1tsp) dried yeast
450g (1lb) strong plain flour
100g (4oz) rye flour
1½ × 5ml tsp (1½tsp) salt
caraway seeds or cummin seeds for sprinkling, optional

This closer-textured bread has good keeping qualities and is delicious with smoked fish and cheese

1 Lightly grease a 22cm (9in) round dish or 900g (2lb) loaf dish and line the base with greaseproof paper.

2 Add the sugar to a third of the water and warm for 30 sec. Stir in the yeast and leave for 8–12 min to activate.

3 Mix the flours and salt well and warm for 30 sec. Warm the remaining liquid for 45 sec.

4 Add the yeast and sufficient of the remaining water to the flours to form a soft dough. Mix well, knead lightly and form into a ball.

5 Place the dough into a bowl covered with clingfilm and prove by heating for 15 sec and leaving to stand for 5–10 min. Repeat this 3–4 times until double in size. If you have the time, knead and prove again.

6 Turn the dough onto a floured surface, knead well until smooth. Shape the dough and place into the prepared container.

7 With a sharp knife, make a cut across the top and widen this by pressing into it with the blade of the knife. Brush the top with oil, sprinkle with rye meal and a few caraway seeds or cummin seeds.

8 Prove as described previously until double in size. Cook for 5½–6½ min, turning once halfway through if necessary. Leave for 10 min before turning out onto a wire rack to cool.

Note: *1½ × 5ml tsp (1½tsp) caraway or cummin seeds may be added to the flours before mixing for a characteristic flavour of rye bread.*

Alternative conventional bake
Place the dough in a greased round ovenware dish or loaf tin. If a metal tin is used, the second proving must be carried out conventionally in a warm place. Cook in a preheated oven at 230°C (450°F) Mark 8 for 15 min, reduce to 190°C (375°F) Mark 5 for 15 min, reduce to 160°C (325°F) Mark 3 for a further 10 min or until cooked through.

Dark rye bread

Follow the ingredients and method for Light Rye Bread using all rye flour.

Light Wholemeal Bread

450g (1lb) plain flour

1 × 5ml tsp (1tsp) salt

1 × 5ml tsp (1tsp) bicarbonate of soda

1 × 5ml tsp (1tsp) cream of tartar

50g (2oz) butter or margarine

350ml (12fl oz) buttermilk or soured milk

Soda bread (*makes 1 loaf*)
POWER SETTING 7 (FULL OR HIGH)

This bread is leavened with soda rather than yeast

1 Lightly grease and flour a 22cm (9in) round dish and line the base with floured, greaseproof paper.
2 Sift the flour, salt and raising agents into a bowl. Rub in the butter finely.
3 Add the milk and mix to a soft dough. Knead lightly on a floured surface and shape or roll into a large round about 2.5cm (1in) thick.
4 Place the dough into the prepared dish and sprinkle the top with flour. Score or cut into 8 wedges.
5 Cook for 5 min, turn the dish, cook for 1–2 min. Leave for 10–15 min before turning out to cool on wire rack.

Alternative conventional bake
Cook in a round ovenware dish or tin in a preheated oven at 200°C (400°F) Mark 6 for 25–30 min.

Brown soda bread

Follow the ingredients and method for Soda Bread substituting 225g ($\frac{1}{2}$lb) of wholemeal flour for white flour.

Fly bread

Follow the ingredients and method for Soda Bread adding 50g (2oz) currants and 25g (1oz) caster sugar to the dry ingredients.

275g (10oz) plain flour

175g (6oz) rolled oats

1 × 5ml tsp (1tsp) salt

1 × 5ml tsp (1tsp) bicarbonate of soda

1 × 5ml tsp (1tsp) cream of tartar

100g (4oz) butter or margarine

1 × 15ml tbsp (1tbsp) caster sugar

275ml ($\frac{1}{2}$pt) buttermilk or soured milk, approximately

rolled oats for sprinkling

Oatmeal bread (*makes 1 loaf*)
POWER SETTING 7 (FULL OR HIGH)

1 Lightly grease a 22cm (9in) round dish and line the base with greaseproof paper; sprinkle with oats.
2 Sift flour, mix in the oats, salt and raising agents. Rub in the butter finely, mix in the sugar.
3 Add sufficient of the milk to mix to a light scone dough. Knead lightly on a floured surface and shape into a round about 2.5cm (1in) thick.
4 Place into the prepared container. Score or cut into 8 wedges and sprinkle the top with oats.
5 Cook for 5 min, turning once halfway through. If necessary, test with a skewer and give an extra minute if not quite cooked.
6 Leave for 10–15 min before turning onto a wire rack to cool.

Alternative conventional bake
Cook in a round ovenware dish or tin in a preheated oven at 200°C (400°F) Mark 6 for 30–35 min.

1 short, crusty French stick

150g (5oz) butter, softened

3–4 cloves garlic, crushed or finely chopped *or*

1–1$\frac{1}{2}$ × 5ml tsp (1–1$\frac{1}{2}$tsp) garlic powder

Garlic bread
POWER SETTING 7 (FULL OR HIGH)

Delicious to serve as a snack or as an accompaniment to a meal

1 Cut the loaf, not quite through, into slices 2.5cm (1in) thick.
2 Cream the butter and beat in the garlic.

3 Spread a large knob of butter between the slices.
4 Protect the thin ends of the loaf with small, smooth pieces of aluminium foil.
5 Place on kitchen paper in the microwave cooker and cover with a piece of damp kitchen paper.
6 Cook for 1½ min or until butter has just melted and bread is warmed through.

Alternative conventional bake
Wrap bread in foil and cook in a preheated oven at 200°C (400°F) Mark 6 for approximately 10 min.

Herb bread

Follow ingredients and method for Garlic Bread substituting 1 × 15ml tbsp (1tbsp) finely chopped fresh mixed herbs or 2 × 5ml tsp (2tsp) dried mixed herbs for the garlic.

Onion bread *(makes 1 loaf)*
POWER SETTING 7 (FULL OR HIGH)

Delicious when eaten with salad or hot soup

1 × 5ml tsp (1tsp) sugar
375ml (12fl oz) water
2 × 5ml tsp (2tsp) dried yeast
450g (1lb) plain flour
1 × 5ml tsp (1tsp) salt
40g (1½oz) butter or margarine
3 × 15ml tbsp (3tbsp) dried onion soup mix

1 Lightly grease a 15cm (6in) soufflé dish and line base with greaseproof paper.
2 Add sugar to half the water and warm for 30 sec. Stir in the yeast and leave to activate for 8–12 min.
3 Sift the flour and salt and warm for 30 sec. Rub in the butter finely, stir in the onion soup mix, reserving 2 × 5ml tsp (2tsp). Warm the rest of the water for 30 sec.
4 Add the yeast and warm water to the flour. Mix well and knead until smooth.
5 Place the dough in a bowl and cover with clingfilm. Prove by heating for 15 sec and leaving to rest for 5–10 min. Repeat 3–4 times until double in size.
6 Knead on a floured surface, shape the dough and place in the prepared container. Prove as described previously and when double in size lightly oil the top and sprinkle with the remaining soup mix.
7 Cook for 5 min, turning once halfway through if necessary. Leave for 10–15 min before removing onto a wire rack to cool.

Alternative conventional bake
Place the dough in a greased, ovenproof dish or 450g (1lb) loaf tin. If a metal tin is used, the second proving must be carried out conventionally in a warm place. Cook in a preheated oven at 200°C (400°F) Mark 6 for about 45 min.

1 × 5ml tsp (1tsp) sugar
275ml (½pt) water
1 × 5ml tsp (1tsp) dried yeast
450g (1lb) plain flour
1 × 5ml tsp (1tsp) salt
½ × 5ml tsp (½tsp) dried mustard
½ × 5ml tsp (½tsp) pepper
175g (6oz) cheddar cheese finely grated
1 × 5ml tsp (1tsp) celery salt, optional

Cheese bread *(makes 1 loaf)*
POWER SETTING 7 (FULL OR HIGH)

1 Dampen the inside of a 15cm (6in) soufflé dish and sprinkle with 1 × 15ml tbsp (1tbsp) of the finely grated cheese. There is no need to grease the dish.
2 Add the sugar to half the water and warm for 30 sec. Stir in the yeast and leave to activate for 8–12 min.
3 Sift the flour and seasonings and warm for 30 sec. Warm the rest of the water for 30 sec.
4 Reserving 1 × 15ml tbsp (1tbsp), stir the rest of the cheese into the flour. Add the yeast and warm water. Mix well and knead until dough is smooth.
5 Place dough in a bowl, cover with clingfilm and prove by heating for 15 sec and leaving to stand for 5–10 min. Repeat until double in size.
6 Knead on a floured surface, shape the dough and place in the prepared container. Prove as described previously until doubled in size. Sprinkle the top with the remaining cheese and celery salt.
7 Cook for 5–6 min, turning once halfway through if necessary.
8 Leave for 10–15 min before turning out onto a wire rack to cool.

Alternative conventional bake
Place the dough in a greased, ovenproof dish or 450g (1lb) loaf tin. If a metal tin is used, the second proving must be carried out conventionally in a warm place. Cook in a preheated oven at 200°C (400°F) Mark 6 for approximately 45 min.

Teatime breads and scones

100g (4oz) plain flour
100g (4oz) wholemeal flour
1½ × 5ml tsp (1½tsp) baking powder
½ × 5ml tsp (½tsp) bicarbonate of soda
1 × 5ml tsp (1tsp) salt
50g (2oz) butter or margarine
175g (6oz) caster sugar
150ml (¼pt) orange juice
2 × 15ml tbsp (2tbsp) grated orange rind
1 egg, beaten
milk for mixing
100g (4oz) walnuts, chopped

Orange nut bread *(makes 1)*
POWER SETTING 7 (FULL OR HIGH)

1 Lightly grease a 15cm (6in) soufflé dish or 900g (2lb) microwave loaf dish and line base with greaseproof paper.
2 Sift flours, raising agents and salt. Rub in the butter finely and stir in the sugar.
3 Mix the orange juice, threequarters of the orange rind and egg and pour into the dry ingredients. Mix well together, adding a little milk if necessary to make a soft mixture. Stir in the walnuts.
4 Turn into the prepared container and cook for 6–7 min, turning once halfway through if necessary.
5 Leave for 10–15 min to cool before turning out onto a wire rack. Sprinkle top with remaining grated orange rind.
6 Serve warm or cold, sliced and buttered.

Alternative conventional bake
Place in a greased and floured 900g (2lb) loaf tin. Cook in a preheated oven at 180°C (350°F) Mark 4 for 1–1¼ hours.

Banana teabread (*makes 1*)
POWER SETTING 7 (FULL OR HIGH)

1 Lightly grease a 15 cm (6in) soufflé dish or 900g (2lb) microwave loaf dish and line the base with greaseproof paper.
2 Sift the flour, bicarbonate of soda and salt. Rub in the butter finely and stir in the sugar. Mash the bananas.
3 Stir in the egg, bananas and threequarters of the nuts, mixing well together. Add a little milk if necessary to make a soft mixture.
4 Turn into the prepared container and cook for 5–6 min, turning once halfway through if necessary.
5 Leave for 10–15 min before turning out onto wire rack. Sprinkle top with remaining walnuts.
6 Serve warm or cold, sliced and buttered.

Alternative conventional bake
Place in a greased and floured 900g (2lb) loaf tin. Cook in a preheated oven at 180°C (350°F) Mark 4 for 1–1¼ hours.

175g (6oz) self-raising flour
⅛ × 5ml tsp (⅛tsp) bicarbonate of soda
¼ × 5ml tsp (¼tsp) salt
40g (1½oz) butter or margarine
75g (3oz) caster sugar
1 egg, beaten
175g (6oz) bananas, peeled weight
75g (3oz) walnuts, chopped
milk for mixing

Date bread (*makes 1*)
POWER SETTING 6 (ROAST OR MEDIUM/HIGH)

1 Lightly grease a 15cm (6in) soufflé dish or 900g (2lb) microwave loaf dish and line the base with greaseproof paper.
2 Heat the butter and sugar in the milk and water for 1½–2 min. Stir until the sugar is dissolved and the butter melted.
3 Sift the flours, salt and bicarbonate of soda and stir whilst pouring in the liquid ingredients and the egg. Mix well until smooth then add the dates.
4 Pour into the prepared container and cook on variable power control setting 6 (roast or medium/high) for 10–12 min, turning once halfway through if necessary.
5 Leave for 10–15 min before turning out and placing on cooling rack. Brush top with apricot glaze.
6 Serve warm or cold, sliced and buttered.

Alternative conventional bake
Place in a greased and floured 900g (2lb) loaf tin. Cook in a preheated oven at 180°C (350°F) Mark 4 for 55–65 min.

50g (2oz) butter or margarine
175g (6oz) dark soft brown sugar
150ml (¼pt) milk and water, mixed
100g (4oz) plain flour
100g (4oz) wholemeal flour
½ × 5ml tsp (½tsp) salt
1 × 5ml tsp (1tsp) bicarbonate of soda
1 egg, beaten
75g (3oz) stoned dates, roughly chopped
Apricot Glaze for top (page 149)

Malt teabread (*makes 1*)
POWER SETTING 7 (FULL OR HIGH)

1 Lightly grease a 15cm (6in) soufflé dish and line the base with greaseproof paper.
2 Sift the flour and salt, rub in the butter finely and stir in the sugar.
3 Warm the milk, golden syrup and malt together for 15 sec, stir until blended. Add to the flour with the egg. Mix well until smooth, adding a little more milk if necessary to give a soft, sticky mixture. Stir in the raisins.
4 Turn the mixture into the prepared container and cook for 4–5 min, turning once halfway through if necessary.
5 Leave for 10–15 min before placing on a cooling rack. When cold, brush top and sides with apricot glaze.
6 Serve cold, sliced and buttered.

175g (6oz) self-raising flour
¼ × 5ml tsp (¼tsp) salt
50g (2oz) butter or margarine
25g (1oz) dark soft brown sugar
2 × 15ml tbsp (2tbsp) milk
2 × 15ml tbsp (2tbsp) golden syrup
2 × 15ml tbsp (2tbsp) malt
1 egg, beaten
100g (4oz) seedless raisins
Apricot Glaze (page 149)

Alternative conventional bake
Place in a greased and floured 900g (2lb) loaf tin. Cook in a preheated oven at 180°C (350°F) Mark 3 for 1–1¼ hours.

225g (½lb) self-raising flour
½ × 5ml tsp (½tsp) salt
½ × 5ml tsp (½tsp) baking powder
75g (3oz) white shortening or lard
175g (6oz) caster sugar
1 egg, beaten
150ml (¼pt) milk, approximately
Marmalade Topping

Quick coffee bread *(makes 1)*
POWER SETTING 7 (FULL OR HIGH)

This goes well served warm with coffee

1 Lightly grease a 18.75cm (7½in) cake dish and line the base with grease-proof paper.
2 Sift the flour, salt and baking powder into a bowl, rub in the fat finely and stir in the sugar.
3 Add the egg with sufficient milk to make a very soft mixture. Beat thoroughly.
4 Turn the mixture into the prepared container and cook until the mixture is risen and the top is just set (approximately 4 min). Sprinkle with the prepared topping and continue to cook for 1½–2 min.
5 Leave until nearly cold before removing from the dish.
6 Serve warm cut into wedges.

Alternative conventional bake
Place mixture into a lightly greased and floured cake dish or tin and cook in a preheated oven at 190°C (375°F) Mark 5 until risen and the top is set (approximately 30–35 min). Sprinkle with the prepared topping and cook for a further 15–20 min.

50g (2oz) plain flour
50g (2oz) soft brown sugar
1 × 15ml tbsp (1tbsp) butter, melted
2 × 5ml tsp (2tsp) milk
2 × 15ml tbsp (2tbsp) dark marmalade

Marmalade topping

Mix all the ingredients together until it resembles coarse breadcrumbs.

Variation
Streusel topping as for Streusel Cake (page 44)

1 × 5ml tsp (1tsp) soft brown sugar
150ml (¼pt) milk
2 × 5ml tsp (2tsp) dried yeast
100g (4oz) wholemeal flour
100g (4oz) strong white flour
1 × 5ml tsp (1tsp) salt
40g (1½oz) butter or margarine
1 × 15ml tbsp (1tbsp) dark soft brown sugar
50g (2oz) currants
50g (2oz) sultanas
25g (1oz) chopped peel
2 × 15ml tbsp (2tbsp) malt
½ × 15ml tbsp (½tbsp) black treacle
Apricot Glaze (page 149)

Malt loaf *(makes 1)*
POWER SETTING 7 (FULL OR HIGH)

1 Lightly grease and line base of a 15cm (6in) soufflé dish or 900g (2lb) microwave loaf dish.
2 Add 1 × 5ml tsp (1tsp) sugar to half the milk and warm for 15–20 sec. Stir in the yeast and leave to activate for 8–12 min.
3 Sift the flours and salt into a bowl and warm for 15–20 sec. Rub in the butter or margarine finely and stir in the brown sugar. Add the currants, sultanas and chopped peel.
4 Add the malt and black treacle to the rest of the milk and warm for 30 sec. Add to the flours with the yeast and mix well together until dough is smooth.
5 Place in the prepared container. Brush the top of the dough lightly with the oil and cover dish with clingfilm.
6 Prove by heating for 15 sec and allowing to stand for 5–10 min. Repeat until double in size. (This rich mixture may take longer to rise).
7 Remove the clingfilm and cook for 4–5 min.
8 Leave for 5–10 min before turning onto a cooling rack. Whilst still warm,

brush top and sides with hot apricot glaze.
9 Slice when cold and serve with butter.

Note: *This loaf improves if kept wrapped for a day before serving.*

Alternative conventional bake
Place in a greased soufflé dish or loaf dish (not metal) and after proving in the microwave, cook in a preheated oven 230°C (450°F) Mark 8 for 10 min, reduce to 190°C (375°F) Mark 5 for 25–30 min. Alternatively, prove in a metal container in a warm place, then cook as above.

Muffins *(makes 12)*
POWER SETTING 7 (FULL OR HIGH)

1 × 5ml tsp (1tsp) sugar
425ml (¾pt) milk
3 × 5ml tsp (3tsp) dried yeast
675g (1½lb) plain flour
1 × 5ml tsp (1tsp) salt

Muffins are normally cooked on a girdle using crumpet rings to hold the dough mixture, but they can also be cooked in the oven. These muffins are cooked in a microwave muffin dish but could also be cooked in the browning dish in the same way as the girdle scones (page 38)

1 Lightly flour a 6-ring microwave muffin dish.
2 Add the sugar to a third of the milk and warm for 30 sec. Stir in the yeast and leave 8–12 min to activate. Warm the rest of the milk for 30 sec.
3 Sift the flour and salt, add the yeast and the milk and mix to a soft dough. Knead lightly on a floured surface and place dough in a bowl and cover with clingfilm.
4 Prove by heating for 15 sec and leaving for 5–10 min. Repeat 3–4 times until the dough is double in size.
5 Knead the dough again and divide into 12 even size pieces. Knead each piece and shape to fit the muffin rings.
6 Place 6 pieces into the muffin pan and dust the tops with flour. Prove slightly by heating for 15 sec and leave for 5 min.
7 Cook for 3–4 min, turning once halfway through if necessary. Leave to cool on wire rack.
8 Repeat with remaining 6 pieces of dough.
9 To serve, split in half, toast each side and butter thickly.

Alternative conventional bake
Place the pieces of dough in crumpet rings and cook slowly on a girdle for 10–12 min, turning over once halfway through. Alternatively cook in a preheated oven at 190°C (375°F) Mark 5 for 20–25 min. To serve, toast on both sides, split and butter thickly.

Devonshire splits *(makes 16)*
POWER SETTING 7 (FULL OR HIGH)

1 Add 1× 5ml tsp (1tsp) sugar to half the milk and warm for 30 sec. Stir in the yeast and leave to activate for 8–12 min.
2 Sift the flour and salt and warm for 30 sec.
3 Add the butter and remaining sugar to the rest of the milk and heat for 1 min, stir until the sugar is dissolved and the butter melted. Add to the flour with the yeast.
4 Mix well and knead until the dough is smooth.
5 Place dough into a bowl, cover with clingfilm and prove by heating for 15 sec and leaving for 5–10 min. Repeat until dough is double in size.
6 Turn onto a lightly floured surface and knead again. Divide into 16 even-sized pieces. Knead each piece, shape and place on the lightly floured microwave shelf. Cover with a piece of clingfilm.
7 Prove as described previously until double in size.
8 Remove clingfilm and rearrange 8 on the shelf.
9 Cook 8 at a time for 2–2½ min. Leave to cool on wire rack. Repeat with remaining 8 pieces.
10 When cold, cut diagonally into each piece and fill with jam and cream. Dust tops with icing sugar.

Alternative conventional bake
After proving, place on lightly greased and floured baking trays and cook in a preheated oven at 220°C (425°F) Mark 7 for 15–20 min.

Fruit buns *(makes 12)*

Follow the ingredients and method for Devonshire Splits adding mixed spice to taste with the flour and working 100g (4oz) mixed dried fruit into the dough at the second kneading stage. Divide the dough into 12 even-sized pieces and prove in the usual way covered with clingfilm. Remove clingfilm and cook 6 at a time for 2½–3 min. Whilst still warm, brush tops with Apricot Glaze (page 149). Alternatively, serve split, toasted and buttered.

Iced buns *(makes 12)*

Cook the Fruit Buns and when cold, coat with Glacé or Soft Icing (page 150).

Bun ring *(cuts into 8–12 wedges)*

Prepare as for Fruit Buns but shape the dough into a circle to fit a lightly greased 20–22.5cm (8–9in) flan dish. Score or cut across into 8–12 wedges. Prove, covered with clingfilm in the usual way. Cook for 4–5 min.
Serve brushed with Apricot Glaze, iced, or toasted and buttered as for Fruit or Iced Buns.

Note: *If freezing the buns, do not ice before freezing. Finish and decorate just before serving.*

1 × 5ml tsp (1tsp) sugar
275ml (½pt) milk
1 × 5ml tsp (1tsp) dried yeast
450g (1lb) plain flour
1 × 5ml tsp (1tsp) salt
50g (2oz) butter
25g (1oz) sugar
whipped cream
jam
icing sugar for sprinkling

(left to right) *Malt Teabread, Date Bread and Malt Loaf*

450g (1lb) White Bread
Dough (page 23)

25g (1oz) butter

150g (5oz) currants

50g (2oz) soft brown sugar

soft brown sugar for
sprinkling

pinch cinnamon or mixed
spice

Apricot Glaze for top (page
149)

Chelsea buns (*makes 8*)
POWER SETTING 7 (FULL OR HIGH)

1 Lightly grease a large shallow dish.
2 Follow the instructions and method for the basic white bread dough until
the end of the first proving.
3 Knead the dough on a floured surface. Roll out to a rectangle approximately 30 × 22.5cm (12 × 9in).
4 Melt the butter for 1 min and brush over the dough. Sprinkle over the
currants and sugar. Roll up from one of the long sides like a swiss roll.
5 Cut into 8 slices and place side by side around the edges and middle of the
prepared container. Prove as before until double in size. Sprinkle with the
sugar and cinnamon or mixed spice.
6 Cook for 6–8 min, turning once halfway through if necessary. Leave to
stand for 5–10 min before removing to cooling rack.
7 Brush with hot Apricot Glaze.

Alternative conventional bake
Place the slices into a large greased shallow dish or tin. If a metal tin is used,
the second proving must be carried out conventionally in a warm place. Cook
in a preheated oven at 220°C (425°F) Mark 7 for 20–25 min.

225g (½lb) plain flour

pinch salt

1 × 15ml tbsp (1tbsp) baking
powder

50g (2oz) butter or margarine

1 × 5ml tsp (1tsp) sugar

150ml (¼pt) milk or milk and
water mixed

oil

Girdle scones (*makes 8–10*)
POWER SETTING 7 (FULL OR HIGH)

*Traditionally cooked on a girdle, these microwave 'girdle' scones are cooked in a
browning dish*

1 Sift flour, salt and baking powder into a bowl. Rub in the butter or
margarine finely. Stir in the sugar and mix to a manageable soft dough with
the milk.
2 Knead lightly on a floured surface and roll into a round approximately
6mm (¼in) thick. Cut into rounds with a 5cm (2in) cutter or cut the large
round into 8 triangles.
3 Preheat the browning dish for 4–5 min, depending on size. Lightly brush
the base with oil.
4 Quickly place the scones into the browning dish, arranging the triangles
with the pointed ends towards the centre.
5 Cook for 1 min, turn the scones over and the dish round, cook for 1½–2
min.
6 Leave to cool on wire rack. Serve hot or cold, split and buttered.

Alternative conventional bake
Cook slowly on a lightly greased girdle for 10–12 min, turning scones over
once halfway through.

Sultana girdle scones (*makes 8–10*)

Follow the ingredients and method for Girdle Scones, adding 2 × 15ml
heaped tbsp (2 heaped tbsp) sultanas to the dry ingredients.

Cheesy girdle scones (*makes 8–10*)

Follow the ingredients and method for Girdle Scones, omitting the sugar and
adding 50g (2oz) grated cheddar cheese to the dry ingredients.

Fruity girdle scones (*makes 8–10*)
POWER SETTING 7 (FULL OR HIGH)

Richer, spicier scones!

1 Sift the flour, salt and spices into a bowl, rub in the butter finely. Stir in the sugar and dried fruit.
2 Mix in the egg, adding sufficient milk to make a manageable, soft dough.
3 Continue with the method as for Girdle Scones.

225g (½lb) self-raising flour
pinch salt
½ × 5ml tsp (½tsp) mixed spice
50g (2oz) butter or margarine
50g (2oz) sugar
50g (2oz) mixed dried fruit
1 egg, beaten
milk to mix
oil

Potato girdle scones (*makes 12–16*)
POWER SETTING 7 (FULL OR HIGH)

1 Add salt to taste to the potatoes with the butter. Work in sufficient flour to give a stiff mixture.
2 Knead lightly on a floured surface and roll out to 6mm (¼in) thick. Cut into rounds with a 5cm (2in) cutter or into triangles.
3 Preheat the browning dish for 4–5 min depending on size and lightly brush the base with oil.
4 Quickly place half the scones in the browning dish, cook for 1 min, turn the scones over and the dish round, cook for 1½–2min.
5 Reheat the browning dish for 1–2 min and cook the second batch as described previously.
6 Serve hot, spread with butter.

450g (1lb) potatoes, cooked and mashed
1–2 × 5ml tsp (1–2tsp) salt
50g (2oz) butter
100g (4oz) flour
oil

Note: *If using left-over cold potatoes, heat them through in the microwave after mashing as hot potatoes give lighter scones.*

Alternative conventional bake
Cook slowly on a lightly greased girdle 10–12 min, turning scones over once halfway through.

Treacle girdle scones (*makes 8*)
POWER SETTING 7 (FULL OR HIGH)

1 Sift flour, salt and raising agents. Rub in the butter or margarine finely.
2 Mix treacle with milk, stir into the dry ingredients.
3 Knead lightly on a floured surface and roll or shape into a round about 1.25cm (½in) thick. Cut across making 8 triangles.
4 Preheat the browning dish for 4–5 min depending on size and lightly brush the base with oil.
5 Quickly place the scones in the dish, arranging the triangles with the pointed ends towards the centre.
6 Cook for 1 min, turn the scones over and the dish round, cook for 1½–2 min.
7 Serve hot or cold, split and spread with butter.

275g (10oz) plain flour
½ × 5ml tsp (½tsp) salt
1 × 5ml tsp (1tsp) bicarbonate of soda
1 × 5ml tsp (1tsp) cream of tartar
50g (2oz) butter or margarine
2 × 15ml tbsp (2tbsp) black treacle
150ml (¼pt) sour or fresh milk
oil

Alternative conventional bake
Cook slowly on a lightly greased girdle 12–14 min, turning scones over once halfway through.

100g (4oz) plain flour

$\frac{1}{4}$ × 5ml tsp ($\frac{1}{4}$tsp) bicarbonate of soda

$\frac{1}{4}$ × 5ml tsp ($\frac{1}{4}$tsp) cream of tartar

$\frac{1}{4}$ × 5ml tsp ($\frac{1}{4}$tsp) salt

25g (1oz) lard or butter

25g (1oz) sugar

40g (1$\frac{1}{2}$oz) currants

1 egg, beaten

milk for mixing

oil

Singin' hinnie (*cuts into 6*)
POWER SETTING 7 (FULL OR HIGH)

This is a girdle cake from Northumberland, so called because it traditionally sizzles ('sings') as it cooks

1 Sift flour, raising agents and salt into a bowl. Rub in the lard or butter finely, add the sugar and currants. Mix well together.
2 Add the egg and sufficient milk to give a soft manageable dough.
3 Knead on a floured surface and roll or shape into a round, about 1.25cm ($\frac{1}{2}$in) thick.
4 Preheat the browning dish for 3$\frac{1}{2}$–4 min, depending on size, and lightly brush the base with oil.
5 Quickly place the cake into the browning dish, cook for 1$\frac{1}{2}$–2 min, turn the cake over and the dish round, cook for 1–1$\frac{1}{2}$ min.
6 Cool, split in half horizontally, butter and sandwich together again. Serve while still warm.

Alternative conventional bake
Cook slowly on a lightly greased girdle for about 10 min, turning over once halfway through.

175g (6oz) self-raising flour

pinch salt

1 × 5ml tsp (1tsp) mixed spice

$\frac{1}{2}$ × 5ml tsp ($\frac{1}{2}$tsp) baking powder

40g (1$\frac{1}{2}$oz) butter or margarine

2 × 5ml tsp (2tsp) sugar

milk for mixing

Spicy scone round (*cuts into 6*)
POWER SETTING 7 (FULL OR HIGH)

1 Lightly grease a 17.5cm (7in) round flan dish and line base with grease-proof paper.
2 Sift flour, salt, mixed spice and baking powder, rub in the butter or margarine finely.
3 Stir in sugar and sufficient milk to make a soft manageable dough. Knead lightly on a floured surface.
4 Roll out to about 1.25cm ($\frac{1}{2}$in) thick. Using a 6.25cm (2$\frac{1}{2}$in) cutter, cut into 6 rounds.
5 Place 5 round the outside edge of the container and 1 in the centre.
6 Cook for 2 min, turn, cook for 1–2 min.
7 Serve hot or cold, split and spread with butter.

Alternative conventional bake
Place rounds in a lightly greased oven dish or tin. Cook in a preheated oven at 200°C (400°F) Mark 6 for 20–30 min.

Iced scone round

Follow the ingredients and method for Spicy Scone Round. When cooked and cool, decorate the top of the scone round with Glacé Icing (page 150), quartered glacé cherries and a sprinkling of chopped almonds or walnuts.

Note: *Do not freeze the scone round when iced and decorated.*

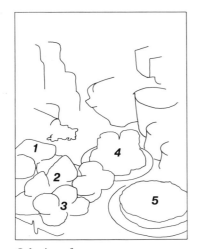

Selection of scones
1 *Treacle Girdle Scones*
2 *Girdle Scones*   3 *Fruity Girdle Scones*   4 *Wholemeal Scones*
5 *Singin' Hinnie*

175g (6oz) self-raising flour
½ × 5ml tsp (½tsp) salt
½ × 5ml tsp (½tsp) baking powder
pinch pepper
¼ × 5ml tsp (¼tsp) dry mustard
40g (1½oz) butter or margarine
50g (2oz) cheese, finely grated
milk for mixing
paprika pepper

Cheesy scone round (*cuts into 6 or 8 wedges*)
POWER SETTING 7 (FULL OR HIGH)

1 Lightly grease a 17.5cm (7in) round flan dish and line base with grease-proof paper.
2 Sift the flour, salt, baking powder and seasonings into a bowl, rub in the butter or margarine finely.
3 Reserve 1 × 15ml tbsp (1tbsp) of the cheese. Stir the remainder into the flour with sufficient milk to mix to a soft manageable dough. Knead lightly on a floured surface.
4 Roll out into a round approximately 17.5cm (7in) diameter. Place into the prepared container. Score to half the depth into 6 or 8 wedges.
5 Cook for approximately 5 min, turning the dish once halfway through.
6 When cooked, sprinkle with the reserved grated cheese mixed with paprika pepper to taste.
7 Split into wedges and serve hot or cold with butter.

Alternative conventional bake
Place in a lightly greased oven dish or tin. Cook in a preheated oven at 200°C (400°F) Mark 6 for 20–30 min.

100g (4oz) plain flour
pinch salt
1 × 5ml tsp (1tsp) bicarbonate of soda
1 × 5ml tsp (1tsp) cream of tartar
100g (4oz) wholemeal flour
2 × 5ml tsp (2tsp) sugar
50g (2oz) butter or margarine
150ml (¼pt) buttermilk or fresh milk with 1½ × 5ml tsp (1½tsp) baking powder

Wholemeal scones (*cuts into 6 or 8 wedges*)
POWER SETTING 7 (FULL OR HIGH)

1 Lightly grease a 17.5cm (7in) round flan dish and line base with grease-proof paper.
2 Sift flour, salt, bicarbonate of soda and cream of tartar into a bowl, stir in the wholemeal flour and sugar. Rub in the butter finely.
3 Stir in the buttermilk or fresh milk with baking powder and mix to a soft dough. Knead lightly on a floured surface.
4 Roll out or shape into a round about 17.5cm (7in) in diameter and place in prepared container. Score to half the depth into 6 or 8 wedges. Dust with wholemeal flour.
5 Cook for 4½–5 min. Serve hot or cold split into wedges, with butter.

Alternative conventional bake
Place in a lightly greased oven dish or tin. Cook in a preheated oven at 220°C (425°F) Mark 7 for 15–20 min.

Continental yeast mixtures

Brioche ring (serves 6–8)
POWER SETTING 7 (FULL OR HIGH)

This rich, moist brioche can be served hot in slices with butter for a continental-style breakfast or may be decorated with glacé fruits and soft icing to serve with coffee or tea

1 Lightly butter a 20cm (8in) microwave ring mould.
2 Add 1 × 5ml tsp (1tsp) sugar to the water and warm for 15 sec. Stir in the yeast and leave for 8–12 min to activate.
3 Sift the flour with the salt, add the 1 × 15ml tbsp (1tbsp) sugar and warm for 30 sec. Melt the butter for 2 min.
4 Add the yeast, eggs and butter to the flour and beat well to form a soft, smooth sticky dough.
5 Cover with clingfilm and prove by heating for 15 sec and leaving for 5–10 min. Repeat until well risen.
6 Knead lightly and pour into the prepared container. Cover with clingfilm and prove again as described previously until it rises to within 2.5cm (1in) of the top of the container. This rich dough may take longer to rise.
7 Remove clingfilm and cook for 3½–4 min, turning once halfway through if necessary. Leave for a few minutes before turning onto a cooling rack.
8 Serve hot in slices with butter, or leave until nearly cold, brush with Soft Icing and decorate with a few slices of glacé fruit.

Alternative conventional bake
Place mixture in a well buttered ring mould or tin. If a metal tin is used, the dough must be proved for the second time conventionally in a warm place. Cook in a preheated oven at 200°C (400°F) Mark 6 for 40–50 min.

Note: *If freezing the brioche ring, do not ice before freezing. Finish and decorate just before serving.*

1 × 5ml tsp (1tsp) sugar
3 × 15ml tbsp (3tbsp) water
1 × 5ml tsp (1tsp) dried yeast
225g (½lb) plain flour
½ × 5ml tsp (½tsp) salt
1 × 15ml tbsp (1tbsp) sugar
175g (6oz) butter
2 eggs, beaten
For decoration, optional:
Soft Icing (page 150)
glacé fruits

Kugelhopf (cuts into about 16 slices)
POWER SETTING 7 (FULL OR HIGH)

This is a rich, light-textured yeast cake, usually eaten with coffee

1 Well butter a 20cm (8in) microwave ring mould.
2 Add 1 × 5ml tsp (1tsp) sugar to the milk and warm for 45 sec. Stir in the dried yeast and leave for 8–12 min to activate.
3 Sift the flour and salt, add caster sugar and warm for 30 sec. Melt the butter for 2 min.
4 Add the yeast, butter and eggs to the flour and beat well to form a soft sticky batter adding a little more milk if necessary. Stir in the dried fruit.
5 Press the almonds around the base and sides of the prepared container and carefully pour in the dough mixture.
6 Cover with clingfilm and prove by heating for 15 sec and leaving for 5–10 min. Prove until risen to within 2.5cm (1in) of the top of the container. This richer dough may take longer to rise.
7 Remove clingfilm and cook for 8–9 min, turning dish every 3 min.
8 Leave for a few minutes before turning onto a cooling rack. Dust heavily with icing sugar before serving.

1 × 5ml tsp (1tsp) sugar
225ml (8fl oz) milk, approximately
2 × 5ml tsp (2tsp) dried yeast
350g (¾lb) plain flour
pinch salt
25g (1oz) caster sugar
100g (4oz) butter
2 eggs, beaten
100g (4oz) currants and seedless raisins
25–50g (1–2oz) flaked or split almonds
icing sugar for dusting

Alternative conventional bake
Place mixture in a kugelhopf tin and prove conventionally in a warm place. Cook in a preheated oven 200°C (400°F) Mark 6 for 50–60 min. If the top browns too much, lower the temperature and continue to cook through.

Basic coffee bread dough
POWER SETTING 7 (FULL OR HIGH)

1 × 5ml tsp (1tsp) sugar
200ml (7fl oz) milk, approximately
2 × 5ml tsp (2tsp) dried yeast
450g (1lb) plain flour
large pinch salt
100g (4oz) butter
100g (4oz) caster sugar
2 eggs, beaten

1 Add 1 × 5ml tsp (1tsp) sugar to the milk, warm for 45 sec, stir in the yeast and leave to activate for 8–12 min.
2 Sift the flour and salt, warm for 30 sec, rub in the butter finely and stir in the caster sugar.
3 Add the yeast mixture and eggs to the flour, mix together then beat well, first with a wooden spoon then with your hand until the mixture is smooth.
4 Cover the bowl with clingfilm and prove by heating for 15 sec and leaving for 5–10 min. Repeat until the dough is double in size. Use as directed in the recipes.

Note: *You will find that this very rich dough takes longer to rise than the plainer doughs but it is well worth the effort for flavour and texture.*

Streusel cake *(serves 10–12)*
POWER SETTING 7 (FULL OR HIGH)

450g (1lb) Basic Coffee Bread Dough (above)
For Streusel topping:
25g (1oz) butter
75g (3oz) soft brown sugar
25g (1oz) plain flour
1 × 5ml tsp (1tsp) cinnamon
50g (2oz) walnuts, chopped

1 Lightly grease a 22.5cm (9in) cake dish and line the base with a circle of greaseproof paper.
2 Follow the method for the basic coffee bread dough until the end of the first proving. Prepare the streusel topping.
3 Heat the butter for 1 min, add the remaining ingredients, mixing well together with a fork.
4 Turn the dough onto a well floured surface and knead lightly.
5 Divide the dough in two and shape both halves to fit the container. Place one half into the container and sprinkle with a third of the topping. Place the other half of the dough on top.
6 Cover and prove as for the basic coffee bread dough until well risen. Remove clingfilm and sprinkle with the remaining streusel mixture.
7 Cook for 6–7 min and leave to cool slightly before removing from the dish to a cooling rack.
8 Serve warm or cold cut into wedges.

Alternative conventional bake
Place the dough into a greased oven dish or tin. If a metal tin is used, the second proving must be carried out conventionally in a warm place. Cook in a preheated oven at 200°C (400°F) Mark 6 for 45–50 min, lowering the heat if it begins to brown too quickly.

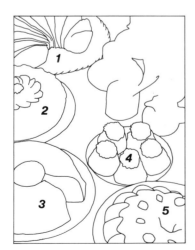

Selection of Coffee Breads
1 Stollen 2 Apple Streusel Cake
3 Kugelhopf 4 Rum Babas
5 Iced Tea Ring

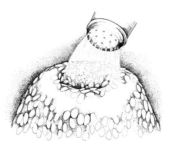

225g (½lb) Basic Coffee Bread
Dough (page 44)
25g (1oz) butter
350g (¾lb) apples, peeled,
cored and thickly sliced
Topping:
as for Streusel Cake (page 44)

Apple streusel cake *(serves 6–8)*
POWER SETTING 7 (FULL OR HIGH)

1 Lightly grease a 20cm (8in) cake dish and line the base with greaseproof paper.
2 Follow the method for the basic coffee bread dough until the end of the first proving.
3 Turn the dough onto a well floured surface and knead lightly. Shape the dough and press into the prepared container. Cover with clingfilm and prove as for basic coffee bread dough until well risen. Remove clingfilm.
4 Melt the butter on a large plate and arrange the apple slices on the plate, turning each slice over so that it is coated in the butter. Cover with clingfilm and cook until just transparent (3–4 min). Drain off the liquid.
5 Prepare the topping as for Streusel Cake.
6 Arrange the apple slices over the dough and sprinkle with the topping.
7 Cook for 4–4½ min, turning the dish once halfway through. Leave for 10–15 min before turning onto a cooling rack.
8 Serve warm or cold cut into wedges.

Alternative conventional bake
Place the dough into a greased oven dish or tin. If a metal tin is used the second proving must be carried out conventionally in a warm place. Cook in a preheated oven at 200°C (400°F) Mark 6 for 40–45 min, lowering the heat if it begins to brown too quickly.

225g (½lb) Basic Coffee Bread
Dough (page 44)
25g (1oz) butter, softened
50g (2oz) caster sugar
50g (2oz) raisins
1 × 5ml tsp (1tsp) cinnamon
For decoration:
Soft or Glacé Icing (page 150)
walnut halves
angelica
glacé cherries

Iced tea ring *(serves 6–8)*
POWER SETTING 7 (FULL OR HIGH)

1 Lightly grease a 20cm (8in) flan dish.
2 Follow the method for the basic coffee bread dough until the end of the first proving.
3 Turn the dough onto a well floured surface, knead lightly and roll out into an oblong approximately 6–12mm (¼–½in) thick.
4 Dab the butter over the dough, sprinkle with raisins and caster sugar mixed with the cinnamon.
5 Roll up like a swiss roll, starting at one of the longer edges.
6 Form into a ring and seal the ends well together. Carefully place the ring into the prepared container (it need not reach the edge of the flan dish as it needs room to rise and spread during proving and cooking).
7 Snip the outside of the ring with scissors, making the cuts about 2.5cm (1in) apart and two thirds of the way into the ring.
8 Cover the dish with clingfilm and prove as for the basic dough until well risen. Remove clingfilm.
9 Cook for 4–4½ min, turning the dish once halfway through. Leave for a few minutes before removing to a cooling rack.
10 Coat the top surface with soft or glacé icing whilst the Tea Ring is still warm, allowing it to dribble down the edges; decorate with walnut halves, pieces of angelica and halved glacé cherries.

Alternative conventional bake
Place the shaped dough into a lightly greased oven dish or on a baking tray. If a metal tin is used, the second proving must be carried out conventionally in a warm place. Cook in a preheated oven at 200°C (400°F) Mark 6 for 25–30 min.

Note: *Do not ice before freezing. Finish and decorate just before serving.*

Stollen (*serves 8–10*)
POWER SETTING 7 (FULL OR HIGH)

1 Lightly grease a 20cm (8in) flan dish.
2 Follow the method for the basic coffee bread dough until the end of the first proving.
3 Turn onto a well floured surface and knead lightly, working in the almonds, cherries, raisins, sultanas and lemon rind.
4 Roll out into an oval about 20 × 25cm (8 × 10in). Melt the butter for 1 min and brush half over the top of the dough.
5 Fold the dough in half lengthwise and form into a crescent to fit the flan dish. Place the dough into the dish and shape the crescent into the edge.
6 Cover with clingfilm and prove as for the basic coffee bread dough until well risen. Remove clingfilm and brush top with remaining butter.
7 Cook for 4 min, turning once halfway through.
8 Leave to cool on wire rack but pour the icing over whilst the Stollen is still warm. Alternatively, dredge with icing sugar when cool.

Alternative conventional bake
Place the shaped dough into a lightly greased oven dish or on a baking tray. If a metal tin is used, the second proving must be carried out conventionally in a warm place. Cook in a preheated oven at 200°C (400°F) Mark 6 for 30–35 min.

Note: *Do not ice before freezing. Finish and decorate just before serving.*

225g ($\frac{1}{2}$lb) Basic Coffee Bread Dough (page 44)
50g (2oz) almonds, blanched and chopped
5 glacé cherries, quartered
25g (1oz) seedless raisins
25g (1oz) sultanas
1 lemon, grated rind
25g (1oz) butter
For decoration:
Soft or Glacé Icing (page 150) or icing sugar

Savarin (*serves 8*)
POWER SETTING 7 (FULL OR HIGH)

1 Lightly grease a 20cm (8in) microwave ring mould.
2 Add the sugar to the water and warm for 30 sec. Stir in the yeast and leave for 8–12 min to activate.
3 Sift the flour and salt and warm for 15 sec. Add the yeast mixture and a little more water if necessary. Mix and knead well; the dough should be fairly soft.
4 Cover and prove by heating for 10 sec and leaving for 5 min. Repeat until double in size.
5 Melt the butter for 1$\frac{1}{2}$ min. Beat the butter and eggs into the dough until it resembles a thick batter. Beat well.
6 Arrange the flaked almonds in the base of the container and carefully pour in the batter.
7 Cover with clingfilm and prove as described earlier until the mixture is well risen in the mould.
8 Remove clingfilm and cook for 6$\frac{1}{2}$–7 min, turning once halfway through.
9 Leave to cool for a few minutes before turning onto a cooling rack.
10 Whilst still warm, pour the syrup over the Savarin and when cool, brush with apricot glaze.
11 To serve, fill the centre with mixed fruit salad and decorate with swirls of whipped cream.

Alternative conventional bake
Place dough in a greased ring mould. If a metal tin is used, the second proving must be carried out conventionally in a warm place. Cook in a preheated oven at 200°C (400°F) Mark 6 for 40 min.

Note: *Do not freeze the Savarin with the fruit salad. Fill and decorate just before serving.*

1 × 5ml tsp (1tsp) sugar
150ml ($\frac{1}{4}$pt) water, approximately
2 × 5ml tsp (2tsp) dried yeast
225g ($\frac{1}{2}$lb) plain flour
$\frac{1}{2}$ × 5ml tsp ($\frac{1}{2}$tsp) salt
50g (2oz) butter or margarine
2 eggs, beaten
25g (1oz) flaked almonds
For serving:
Syrup (page 49)
Apricot Glaze (page 149)
whipped cream
fruit salad

Syrup (for Savarin)
POWER SETTING 7 (FULL OR HIGH)

100g (4oz) caster sugar
150ml (¼pt) water
1 × 5ml tsp (1tsp) lemon juice
2 × 15 ml tbsp (2tbsp) kirsch

1 Add the sugar to the water and heat for 1 min. Stir until the sugar is dissolved. Bring to the boil in the microwave and boil until a thick syrup is formed.
2 Stir in the lemon juice and kirsch and pour over the Savarin whilst warm.

Rum babas (*makes 12*)
POWER SETTING 7 (FULL OR HIGH)

225g (½lb) Savarin mixture (page 47)
50g (2oz) currants
For serving:
Rum Syrup
Apricot Glaze (page 149)
whipped cream

These are individual sweets made from the basic Savarin mixture

1 Lightly grease a 6-ring microwave muffin dish.
2 Follow the method for Savarin until the eggs and butter have been added after the first proving.
3 Reserving half of the currants, place a few into each of the prepared muffin rings and carefully pour in half the batter so that it comes halfway up each ring. Prove as for the Savarin until the mixture is well risen in the moulds.
4 Cook for 3–4 min, turn onto a cooling rack.
5 Repeat with the remaining currants and batter.
6 Soak the babas well in the rum syrup and, when cold, brush with apricot glaze.
7 Serve cold, piped with whipped cream, allowing 1 or 2 per person.

Alternative conventional bake
Divide mixture between 12 small border rings (tin). Prove conventionally in a warm place. Cook in a preheated oven at 220°C (425°F) Mark 7 for 15–20 min.

Rum syrup

Follow the ingredients and method for the Savarin Syrup (above) substituting rum for the kirsch.

Gannat
POWER SETTING 7 (FULL OR HIGH)

1 × 5ml tsp (1tsp) sugar
150ml (¼pt) milk
2 × 5ml tsp (2tsp) dried yeast
275g (10oz) plain flour
¼ × 5ml tsp (¼tsp) salt
pinch pepper
50g (2oz) butter
2 eggs, beaten
100g (4oz) emmenthal or gruyère cheese, finely grated
paprika pepper for sprinkling

A rich cheese bread which makes delicious sandwiches

1 Lightly butter a 17.5–20cm (7–8in) microwave flan dish.
2 Add the sugar to the milk and warm for 30 sec. Stir in the yeast and leave for 8–12 min to activate.
3 Sift the flour and seasonings and warm for 30 sec. Melt the butter for 1–1¼ min.
4 Add the yeast, butter and eggs to the flour and beat well to form a soft sticky dough.
5 Cover with clingfilm and prove by heating for 15 sec and leaving for 5–10 min. Repeat until dough has doubled in size.
6 Knead the dough and work in most of the cheese, reserving 1 × 15ml tbsp (1tbsp). Shape the dough and place in the prepared container.
7 Cover with clingfilm and prove until double in size. Remove clingfilm and sprinkle the top of the dough with the remaining cheese and paprika pepper.
8 Cook for about 5 min, turning once halfway through. Leave to cool for a few minutes before removing onto a cooling rack.

Savarin

9 Serve hot with butter or leave to cool and split in half and sandwich together with cream cheese.

Alternative conventional bake
Place dough in buttered flan dish or sandwich tin. If a metal tin is used, the second proving must be carried out conventionally in a warm place. Cook in a preheated oven at 200°C (400°F) Mark 6 for 50–55 min.

Cakes, traditional and fancy

There are a great variety of recipes to make both plain and richer cakes. Most of them are suitable for cooking in the microwave and all given in this section have those good, light textures and delicious flavours associated with home-baked cakes. The combination of fresh ingredients and the speed of cooking in the microwave result in a cake of which to be proud. The flavour and texture of a cake are dependent upon the ingredients and mixing methods.

Flour

Always use the flour which is recommended in the recipe; for example, do not substitute self-raising flour for plain flour as the success of the recipe may be dependent upon different proportions of raising agents to that present in self-raising flour. Ensure that the flour is kept dry during storage and sift before use with a good pinch of salt for flavour. Sifting aerates the flour and removes any small lumps.

Fats

Butter is a good fat to use in most cake recipes as it improves the flavour, but margarine may be used instead and is easier to cream. If making cakes with soft margarines, always use them directly from the refrigerator and be careful not to overcream, particularly if an electric food mixer is being used to beat the ingredients. Alternatively, try an 'all-in-one' or 'one-stage' cake mixture when using soft margarine (see page 56). White vegetable cooking fats do not have a lot of flavour and so they are best combined with butter or margarine.

Sugar

Caster sugar is best for light cake mixtures as a coarser-grained sugar may result in a cake with a spotted top surface. Granulated can be used for the rubbed-in methods and soft brown sugar gives good flavour and colour to microwave-baked cakes. Demerara sugar is best used in melting methods for gingerbreads and parkins.

Eggs

Eggs are essential to give light textures as they coagulate during cooking, trapping the air which has been beaten into the mixture. Some recipes depend entirely upon the air whisked into the eggs as the raising agent. Provided that the eggs are sufficiently beaten, no other raising agent is required.

Raising agents

Baking powder is a commercially prepared raising agent made from a combination of cream of tartar and bicarbonate of soda in the ratio of 2 : 1 respectively. The baking powder is normally sifted with the flour and, when moistened, the gluten in the flour holds the gas made by the raising agent in the form of tiny bubbles. When heated, the gases expand causing the cake to rise and the gluten to set, thereby holding the air bubbles and giving a light texture to the cooked cake. However, the gluten in the flour is only capable of holding a certain amount of gas and therefore if too much raising agent is

Genoese Sponge Sandwich ready for decoration

Decorated gâteau with Feathered Icing

used, the cake will rise at first and then collapse giving a close-textured, heavy cake.

Fruit and candied peel

Unless clearly marked as cleaned, ready for use, all fruit should be picked over and washed before using. It should be dried in a cloth or teatowel and then spread out on a tray in a warm place to dry slowly. It is important that the fruit is thoroughly dry before using. A light sprinkling of flour taken from the amount required in the recipe can be mixed with the fruit before adding the fruit to the mixture.

For the best flavours buy the larger pieces of candied peel. Remove the sugar and then chop or grate the peel or cut into fine slivers. The peel may be softened first by soaking for a few minutes in hot water. Pre-chopped peel can be used for quickness and convenience.

The fruit cake recipes in this section have been specially developed and tested for cooking in the microwave as generally cakes with a high proportion of fruit do not cook well.

Nuts

Methods of blanching and browning nuts are given in the 'Nuts and Icings' section (page 148).

Mixing methods

Creaming: The creaming method is best suited to most cakes for a smooth, even rise and light texture. All ingredients should be preferably at room temperature to prevent curdling of the mixture. Chilled or frozen butter or margarine may be softened in the microwave for a few seconds before use.

Place the butter or margarine into a bowl, gradually breaking it down with a wooden spoon until it appears creamy. Add the sugar a little at a time, beating well and scraping down the sides of the bowl with a spatula. When the butter and sugar are well creamed together, add the beaten eggs a little at a time, beating the mixture well after each addition. For larger quantities or when using a food mixer, the eggs may be added one at a time.

Take care not to over-cream the butter and sugar, particularly when using a food mixer. If too much air is beaten into the mixture, the cake can rise up during cooking and then sink slightly when cooking is complete. Quite often it is preferable to cream the mixture by hand for a microwave-baked cake.

If the mixture should curdle when adding the eggs, $1 \times 15\text{ml}$ tbsp (1tbsp) of the flour may be beaten in with each addition of the eggs. Then very carefully fold in the sifted flour with a metal spoon, cutting and turning rather than stirring otherwise you may remove the air already beaten into the mixture. Flour may be added with the aid of a food mixer but the slowest speed setting should be used.

Rubbing-in: This method is normally used for plain and small cakes. The flour and salt are sifted into a bowl, then the fat is cut into small pieces and added. It is then rubbed lightly into the flour with the fingertips until it resembles fine breadcrumbs. The mixture should be aerated as much as possible at this stage by lifting and dropping the flour and fatcrumbs as you are rubbing in with the fingertips. The beaten eggs and liquid ingredient are then added to the mixture, beating well. Rubbing in can also be carried out using an electric food mixer on a slow to medium setting.

Melting: This method is used for gingerbreads and parkins and as the texture is usually moist, these cakes have good keeping qualities and usually improve after storing for a day or so in an airtight tin or aluminium foil.

The fat, sugar and liquid ingredients are melted together in the microwave cooker and then added to the flour and spices sifted together. The result is a mixture similar to a thick batter which can easily be poured into the container or dish before cooking.

Dropping consistency

The dropping consistency of a cake mixture helps to determine its texture before cooking. A softer dropping consistency is when the mixture falls fairly easily from the spoon; a stiffer dropping consistency is when the spoonful of mixture needs to be shaken to allow it to drop from the spoon.

Cooking the cake

Wetter cake mixtures are the most successful in the microwave cooker and therefore the liquid quantities given in the recipes may seem greater than you are normally used to. As cakes rise extremely well, the container should not be more than half filled with the uncooked mixture to allow for rising during cooking. If a cake starts to rise unevenly, simply give it a turn every $1\frac{1}{2}$–2 minutes during a 6–minute cooking period. Due to the fact that the centre cooks more slowly than the outside edges, it may be necessary with stiffer or richer cake mixtures to hollow out the middle before cooking, to prevent doming of the top surface. A trussing needle or fine skewer can be inserted into the cake to test whether it is cooked. If the skewer comes out clean and dry, the cake is cooked. However it is always better to remove the cake when it is very slightly moist on top as it will finish setting during its standing time. Do not be impatient and invert the cake too soon onto the cooling rack; it should be left to cool for 5–15 minutes depending on its texture before turning out. To avoid the edges of the cake sticking when it is left to stand and cool in its container, roll it around gently in the container after cooking. This will bring the cake away from the edges and ensure a neat result.

Cakes which are cooked conventionally should be baked in a preheated oven to the temperature recommended in the recipe and on a middle shelf position.

Most cakes can be frozen. Those with special decoration should be open frozen until hard, then wrapped, sealed and labelled before storing.

Biscuits

Not all biscuit mixtures can be baked in the microwave cooker but those recipes given in this section will enable you to achieve success with 'cookie' types and a few specialities. As biscuits are best made in small quantities and eaten quickly, the microwave is ideal. After cooking, allow them to set before removing them to a cooling rack. When cool, store them immediately on their own (never with cakes) in an airtight tin.

Biscuits which are to be cooked conventionally should be placed towards the middle/top of the preheated oven.

When cooking several biscuits or small cakes together in the microwave cooker, they should be arranged in a circle where possible; if some are cooked before others, remove them from the oven, then rearrange and leave the remainder to carry on cooking.

Plain cakes

175g (6oz) butter or
margarine
175g (6oz) caster sugar
3 eggs, beaten
175g (6oz) plain flour
pinch salt
2 × 5ml tsp (2tsp) baking
powder
2 × 15ml tbsp (2tbsp) hot
water
jam or Buttercream (pages 150–
151)
icing sugar for dusting

Victoria sandwich (*cuts into 8*)
POWER SETTING 7 (FULL OR HIGH)

1 Line a 18.75–20cm (7½–8in) cake dish with clingfilm or lightly grease and line base with greaseproof paper.
2 Cream the butter or margarine until soft, add the sugar and beat well together until light and fluffy.
3 Add the eggs gradually, beating well after each addition.
4 Sift the flour, salt and baking powder and fold into the creamed mixture carefully with a metal spoon. Add the hot water and fold into mixture.
5 Turn mixture into the prepared dish and cook for 6½–7½ min. Leave for 5–10 min before placing on cooling rack.
6 When cold, cut in half horizontally and sandwich the two halves together with jam or buttercream. Dust the top with icing sugar.

Alternative conventional bake
Divide the mixture between two greased and floured sandwich tins and cook in a preheated oven at 190°C (375°F) Mark 5 for 25–30 min. Remove from the tins and, when cold, sandwich the sponges together and finish as above.

175g (6oz) soft margarine
175g (6oz) caster sugar
3 eggs, beaten
175g (6oz) self-raising flour
pinch salt
2 × 15ml tbsp (2tbsp) hot
water
jam or Buttercream (pages 150–
151)
icing sugar for dusting

'One stage' victoria sandwich (*cuts into 8*)
POWER SETTING 7 (FULL OR HIGH)

1 Line a 18.75–20cm (7½–8in) cake dish with clingfilm or lightly grease and line base with greaseproof paper.
2 Place all the ingredients except the jam and icing sugar into a bowl and mix until combined, then beat well until smooth.
3 Place mixture into prepared dish, smooth top and cook for 6½–7½ min. Leave for 5–10 min before placing on cooling rack.
4 When cold, cut in half horizontally and sandwich together with jam or buttercream. Dust top with icing sugar.

Alternative conventional bake
Divide the mixture between two greased and floured sandwich tins and cook in a preheated oven at 180°C (350°F) Mark 4 for 35–40 min. Remove from tins and when cold, finish as above.

4 eggs
100g (4oz) caster sugar
100g (4oz) plain flour
pinch salt
jam
whipped cream
icing sugar for dusting

Whisked sponge (*cuts into 8*)
POWER SETTING 7 (FULL OR HIGH)

A light sponge cake which relies on the whisking of air into the eggs as the raising agent, best eaten on the day it is made

1 Line a 18.75–20cm (7½–8in) cake dish with clingfilm, or lightly grease and line base with greaseproof paper.
2 Whisk the eggs and sugar together until trebled in volume and really thick and creamy.
3 Sift the flour and salt and sprinkle over the mixture, very carefully folding in with a metal spoon and turning the mixture over from the base of the bowl to ensure that all the flour is mixed in.

56

4 Pour into the prepared container and cook for 4½–5 min. Leave for 5–10 min before placing on a cooling rack.
5 When cold, cut in half horizontally and sandwich the two halves together with jam and cream. Dust the top with icing sugar.

Alternative conventional bake
Divide the mixture between two greased and floured sandwich tins and cook in a preheated oven at 200°C (400°F) Mark 6 for 15–20 min. Remove from the tins and when cold, sandwich the sponges together and finish as above.

Genoese sponge sandwich *(cuts into 8)*

This cake has better keeping qualities than the Whisked Sponge and makes a good base for various fillings and toppings for richer gâteaux.

Follow the ingredients and method for Whisked Sponge. Melt 50g (2oz) butter for 1–1½ min and add to the thickened mixture with the flour by pouring the melted butter in a thin stream down the side of the bowl whilst folding in the flour and butter with a metal spoon. Fold in very carefully, ensuring that the spoon cuts across the base of the bowl so that all the flour and butter are well mixed in. Cook and decorate as for Whisked Sponge; alternative decorations and fillings are given in recipes in the 'Richer Cakes and Gâteaux' section (page 72).

Basic cake mixture *(cuts into 8)*
POWER SETTING 7 (FULL OR HIGH)

225g (½lb) self-raising flour
pinch salt
100g (4oz) butter or margarine
100g (4oz) soft brown sugar
2 eggs, beaten
few drops lemon juice
milk for mixing
Apricot Glaze, optional (page 149)

1 Line a 18.75–20cm (7½–8in) cake dish with clingfilm or lightly grease and line the base with greaseproof paper.
2 Sift flour and salt, rub in the butter or margarine finely, stir in the sugar.
3 Mix in the eggs, lemon juice and sufficient milk to form a soft dropping consistency.
4 Turn the mixture into the prepared dish and cook for 5½–7 min. Allow to cool slightly before removing from the dish onto a cooling rack.
5 When cold, brush with apricot glaze.

Alternative conventional bake
Place the mixture into a greased and lined cake tin and cook in a preheated oven at 180°C (350°F) Mark 4 for 1–1¼ hrs.

Fruit cake

Follow the ingredients and method for the Basic Cake Mixture adding 150g (5oz) mixed dried fruit to the dry ingredients after the sugar.

Sultana cake

Follow the ingredients and method for the Basic Cake Mixture, adding 150g (5oz) sultanas to the dry ingredients after the sugar.

Orange or lemon cake

Follow the ingredients and method for the Basic Cake Mixture, adding the grated rind and juice of 2 oranges or lemons instead of some of the milk. Decorate with Orange or Lemon Glacé Icing or Buttercream (pages 150–1).

Marmalade cake

Follow the ingredients and method for the Basic Cake Mixture omitting the lemon juice and adding the grated rind of 2 oranges, a few drops of orange colouring and 2 × 15ml tbsp (2tbsp) bitter orange marmalade. Decorate with Orange Glacé Icing (page 150) or Orange Buttercream (page 151).

Banana cake

Follow the ingredients and method for the Basic Cake Mixture adding 2 peeled and mashed bananas to the dry ingredients after the sugar. When cooked and cold, brush the top with Apricot Glaze (page 149).

Coffee cake

Follow the ingredients and method for the Basic Cake Mixture adding coffee essence or instant coffee blended with a little warm water instead of the lemon juice. Decorate with Coffee Glacé Icing (page 150) or Buttercream (pages 150–1) and walnut halves.

Coconut cake

Follow the ingredients and method for the Basic Cake Mixture, adding 175g (6oz) desiccated coconut to the dry ingredients after the sugar; a little more milk for mixing may be required. When cold, decorate with Apricot Glaze or Glacé Icing (page 150) and toasted coconut (page 149).

Almond cake

Follow the ingredients and method for the Basic Cake Mixture, adding 50g (2oz) blanched and chopped almonds to the dry ingredients after the sugar. Omit the few drops of lemon juice and add a little almond essence instead. When cold, brush with Apricot Glaze (page 149) and Toasted Flaked Almonds (page 149).

Note: *Do not freeze the cakes with glacé icing; freeze the basic cake, finish and decorate just before serving.*

(left) *Cherry and Coconut Ring Cake*,
(above right) *Fruit Gingerbread*,
(below) *Coconut Cake*

150g (5oz) black treacle
100g (4oz) golden syrup
100g (4oz) butter or margarine
150ml ($\frac{1}{4}$pt) milk
$\frac{1}{2}$ × 5ml tsp ($\frac{1}{2}$tsp) bicarbonate of soda
100g (4oz) plain flour
pinch salt
$\frac{1}{2}$ × 5ml tsp ($\frac{1}{2}$tsp) ground ginger
25g (1oz) caster sugar
225g ($\frac{1}{2}$lb) rolled oats

Yorkshire parkin (cuts into 8)
POWER SETTING 7 (FULL OR HIGH) AND 6 (ROAST OR MEDIUM/HIGH)

1 Line a 20–22.5cm (8–9in) flan dish with clingfilm.
2 Place treacle, syrup and butter or margarine in a bowl and heat for 2 min, then stir until blended.
3 Warm the milk for 30 sec and stir in the bicarbonate of soda.
4 Sift the flour, salt and ground ginger, stir in the caster sugar and rolled oats.
5 Mix together with the treacle and the milk, beating well until smooth.
6 Pour the mixture into the prepared container and cook on variable power setting 6 (roast or medium/high) for 12–14 min turning every 3 min. Leave to stand until cold.
7 Serve cut into wedges.

Alternative conventional bake
Place mixture in a greased and lined or floured shallow cake tin and cook in a preheated oven at 160°C (325°F) Mark 3 for 45–50 min.

Note: *If your microwave cooker has no variable power control setting, either divide the above mixture in two and cook each separately or make up half quantity. Place in a 17.5cm (7in) cake dish and cook for 4–5 min at normal, full or high setting.*

100g (4oz) butter or margarine
225g ($\frac{1}{2}$lb) black treacle
75g (3oz) soft brown sugar
2 × 15ml tbsp (2tbsp) orange marmalade
150ml ($\frac{1}{4}$pt) milk
$\frac{1}{2}$ × 5ml tsp ($\frac{1}{2}$tsp) bicarbonate of soda
100g (4oz) self-raising flour
2 × 5ml tsp (2tsp) ground ginger
1 × 5ml tsp (1tsp) mixed spice
100g (4oz) wholemeal flour
2 eggs, beaten
Apricot Glaze (page 149)

Sticky gingerbread (cuts into 12–16 wedges)
POWER SETTING 7 (FULL OR HIGH) AND 6 (ROAST OR MEDIUM/HIGH)

1 Line a 22.5cm (9in) cake dish with clingfilm.
2 Place the butter or margarine, treacle, sugar and orange marmalade into a bowl, heat for 2–3 min then stir until blended.
3 Warm the milk for 30 sec and stir in the bicarbonate of soda.
4 Sift the self-raising flour and spices, stir in the wholemeal flour.
5 Add the treacle mixture, milk and eggs to the dry ingredients and mix thoroughly until smooth.
6 Pour the mixture into the prepared dish and cook on variable power control setting 6 (roast or medium/high) for 12–14 min, turning every 3 min.
7 Place on cooling rack and when cool, brush with apricot glaze. Serve cut into wedges.

Alternative conventional bake
Divide mixture between 2 × 900g (2lb) loaf tins which have been greased and floured. Cook in a preheated oven at 160°C (325°F) Mark 3 for 1$\frac{1}{4}$–1$\frac{1}{2}$ hrs.

Fruit gingerbread

Follow the ingredients and method for Sticky Gingerbread, adding 50g (2oz) sultanas or raisins or chopped crystallised ginger or pineapple to the dry ingredients. When cool, brush with apricot glaze and decorate with flaked almonds.

Note: *If your microwave cooker has no variable power control setting, either divide the above mixture into two and cook each separately, or make up half quantity. Place in a 15cm (6in) cake dish and cook for 3$\frac{1}{2}$–4$\frac{1}{2}$ min at normal, full or high setting.*

Cherry and walnut ring cake *(cuts into 8–10)*
POWER SETTING 7 (FULL OR HIGH)

1 Lightly grease a 20cm (8in) microwave ring mould and line base with greaseproof paper or line with clingfilm.
2 Cream the butter or margarine until soft, add the sugar and beat well until light and fluffy.
3 Add the eggs gradually, beating well after each addition.
4 Sift the flour and salt and fold into the creamed mixture with a metal spoon. Add the walnuts and milk, mix well to form a soft mixture.
5 Place the cherries over the base of the container and spoon in the mixture.
6 Cook for 5–6 min, turning once halfway through if necessary. Leave for 10–15 min before turning onto a cooling tray.
7 When cool, dust heavily with icing sugar.

100g (4oz) butter or margarine
100g (4oz) caster sugar
2 eggs, beaten
175g (6oz) self-raising flour
pinch salt
50g (2oz) walnuts, chopped
1–2 × 15ml tbsp (1–2tbsp) milk
100g (4oz) glacé cherries, halved
icing sugar for dusting

Alternative conventional bake
Place mixture into a greased and floured ring mould or tin and cook in a preheated oven at 180°C (350°F) Mark 4 for 1–1¼ hr.

Cherry and coconut ring cake

Follow the ingredients and method for Cherry and Walnut Ring Cake, substituting 50g (2oz) desiccated coconut for the walnuts. More milk will be necessary to make a soft mixture. Decorate with toasted coconut (page 149).

Cherry and almond ring cake

Follow the ingredients and method for Cherry and Walnut Ring Cake, substituting 50g (2oz) ground almonds for the walnuts and adding a few drops of almond essence and a little extra milk. Decorate with toasted flaked almonds (page 149).

Marble cake *(cuts into 8)*
POWER SETTING 7 (FULL OR HIGH)

1 Line a 21.25–22.5cm (8½–9in) cake dish with clingfilm or grease and line base with greaseproof paper.
2 Cream the butter or margarine until soft, add the sugar and beat together until light and fluffy.
3 Add the eggs gradually, beating well after each addition.
4 Sift flour and salt, fold into the creamed mixture with a metal spoon. Divide the mixture between 3 bowls.
5 To one bowl add and mix in the cocoa and water; to the second add a few drops of cochineal to give a good colour; to the third add the vanilla essence.
6 Place spoonfuls of the mixtures into the prepared dish, alternating the colours then lightly swirl them together.
7 Cook for 7–8 min, turning the dish every 2 min.
8 Leave to cool 10–15 min before removing cake to a wire rack.
9 When cold, decorate with feathered glacé icing, or buttercream tinted pale pink and hundreds and thousands.

175g (6oz) butter or margarine
175g (6oz) caster sugar
3 eggs, beaten
225g (½lb) self-raising flour
pinch salt
1 × 15ml tbsp (1tbsp) cocoa blended with a little hot water
few drops cochineal
½ × 5ml tsp (½tsp) vanilla essence
Feathered Glacé Icing (page 150) or Buttercream (pages 150–1) and hundreds and thousands

Alternative conventional bake
Place mixture into a greased and lined or floured cake tin and cook in a preheated oven at 180°C (350°F) Mark 4 for 1¼–1½ hr.

Small cakes and biscuits

Queen cakes *(makes about 24)*
POWER SETTING 7 (FULL OR HIGH)

1 Place 6 paper cake cases into a 6-ring microwave muffin pan.
2 Cream the butter or margarine add the sugar and beat well together until light and fluffy.
3 Add the eggs gradually, beating well after each addition.
4 Sift the flour and salt and toss in the currants. Fold into the creamed mixture with a metal spoon.
5 Mix in sufficient milk to give a soft dropping consistency.
6 Place spoonfuls of the mixture into the paper cases filling them no more than two-thirds full.
7 Cook for 2–2½ min, turning the dish once halfway through.
8 Remove onto a cooling rack and cook the remainder in batches of 6.

Alternative conventional bake
Divide spoonfuls of the mixture between paper cases placed on baking trays and cook in a preheated oven at 190°C (375°F) Mark 5 for 15–20 min.

Variations
Omit the currants and replace with one of the following:
75g (3oz) finely chopped dates
75g (3oz) finely chopped glacé cherries
75g (3oz) polka dots (chocolate chips)
75g (3oz) finely chopped crystallised ginger
75g (3oz) chopped walnuts
75g (3oz) sultanas

175g (6oz) butter or margarine
175g (6oz) caster sugar
3 eggs
175g (6oz) self-raising flour
pinch salt
75g (3oz) currants
milk for mixing
24 paper cases, approximately

Iced cakes *(makes about 24)*
POWER SETTING 7 (FULL OR HIGH)

1 Place 6 paper cake cases into a 6-ring microwave muffin pan.
2 Follow the ingredients and method for the Basic Cake Mixture.
3 Place spoonfuls of the mixture into the cake cases, filling them each about two-thirds full.
4 Cook for about 2 min, turning the dish once halfway through.
5 Place onto a cooling rack and cook the remaining mixture in batches of 6.
6 To finish, coat tops with soft or glacé icing and top with glacé cherry and slivers of angelica.

Alternative conventional bake
Divide spoonfuls of the mixture between paper cases placed on baking trays. Cook in a preheated oven at 190°C (375°F) Mark 5 for 15–20 min.

Note: *If freezing these cakes, do not ice before freezing. Decorate just before serving.*

225g (½lb) Basic Cake Mixture (page 57)
Soft or Glacé Icing (page 150)
glacé cherries, halved
angelica
24 paper cases, approximately

Marble Cake

63

75g (3oz) self-raising flour

25g (1oz) cocoa

pinch salt

50g (2oz) butter or margarine

50g (2oz) soft brown sugar

1 egg, beaten

120ml (4fl oz) milk, approximately

Chocolate Fudge Icing (page 152) or melted chocolate hazelnuts, optional

16 paper cases, approximately

Chocolate cup cakes *(makes 12–16)*
POWER SETTING 7 (FULL OR HIGH)

1 Place 6 paper cases into a 6-ring microwave muffin pan.
2 Sift the flour, cocoa and salt into a bowl. Rub in the butter or margarine finely, stir in the sugar.
3 Mix in the egg and the milk to form a very soft, almost runny mixture.
4 Half fill the paper cases with the mixture and cook for 2 min, turning the dish after 1 min.
5 Remove onto a cooling rack and cook the remainder in batches of 6.
6 When cold, coat the top of each cake with chocolate fudge icing or melted chocolate. Decorate with a hazelnut on the top of each cake.

Alternative conventional bake
Divide the mixture between paper cases placed on baking trays. Cook in a preheated oven at 190°C (375°F) Mark 5 for 15–20 min.

Note: *Do not ice before freezing. Decorate just before serving.*

100g (4oz) butter

100g (4oz) caster sugar

2 eggs, beaten

100g (4oz) self-raising flour

pinch salt

1 × 15ml tbsp (1tbsp) hot water

4 × 15ml tbsp (4tbsp) red jam, warmed

1 × 15ml tbsp (1tbsp) water

3 × 15ml tbsp (3tbsp) desiccated coconut

4–5 glacé cherries

angelica

Madeleines *(makes 8–10)*
POWER SETTING 7 (FULL OR HIGH)

1 Lightly grease a 6-ring microwave muffin pan.
2 Cream the butter, add the sugar and beat well together until light and fluffy. Add the eggs gradually, beating well after each addition.
3 Sift the flour and salt and fold into the creamed mixture with a metal spoon. Mix in the hot water.
4 Place the mixture into the moulds, not filling more than two-thirds full.
5 Cook for 2–2½ min, turning the dish once halfway through. Leave for a few minutes before inverting onto a cooling rack.
6 Repeat with the remaining mixture.
7 Heat the jam and water and boil for 1 min.
8 When the madeleines are cold, brush with jam and roll in the coconut. Decorate with halved glacé cherries and slivers of angelica.

Alternative conventional bake
Divide mixture between 8–10 greased dariole moulds placed on a baking tray. Cook in a preheated oven at 180°C (350°F) Mark 4 for 20–25 min.

Rum truffle cakes *(makes about 12)*
POWER SETTING 7 (FULL OR HIGH)

These are delicious and are quick and easy to make; the mixture is quite rich so smaller ones could be made for Petits Fours to serve with coffee after a meal

1 Melt the butter and chocolate for 1½–2 min. Stir until well blended.
2 Add all the remaining ingredients except the vermicelli and mix well together. If the mixture is too dry, add a little more jam or rum. If it is too wet, add a few more cake crumbs.
3 Allow mixture to cool before forming into balls and rolling in the chocolate vermicelli or desiccated coconut.
4 Place in decorative paper cake cases before serving.

50g (2oz) butter
100g (4oz) plain chocolate
275g (10oz) cake crumbs, approximately
75g (3oz) icing sugar, sifted
75g (3oz) seeded raisins, finely chopped
75g (3oz) glacé cherries, finely chopped
3 × 15ml tbsp (3tbsp) apricot jam, sieved
2 × 15ml tbsp (2tbsp) rum *or* 2 × 5ml tsp (2tsp) rum essence
chocolate vermicelli or desiccated coconut for coating

Swiss tartlets *(makes 6)*
POWER SETTING 4 (DEFROST OR MEDIUM)

1 Place 6 paper cake cases into a 6-ring microwave muffin pan.
2 Soften the butter and add the sifted icing sugar. Beat together until light and fluffy, beat in the vanilla essence.
3 Sift the flour and salt and add to the creamed mixture gradually, beating well after each addition.
4 Place the mixture into a large piping bag fitted with a large star nozzle and pipe the mixture into the paper cases. Start at the centre and pipe in a spiral motion round the sides, leaving a slight depression in the centre.
5 Cook on setting 4 (defrost or medium) for 7–8 min, turning every 1½ min.
6 Leave to cool on wire rack. Dredge with icing sugar and place a little redcurrant jelly in the centre of each tartlet.

100g (4oz) butter
25g (1oz) icing sugar, sifted
1 × 5ml tsp (1tsp) vanilla essence
100g (4oz) plain flour
pinch salt
icing sugar for dusting
a little redcurrant jelly

Alternative conventional bake
Pipe the mixture into paper cases on a baking tray. Cook in a preheated oven at 180°C (350°F) Mark 4 until just set and pale in colour.

Flapjacks *(cuts into 8 wedges)*
POWER SETTING 7 (FULL OR HIGH)

1 Line a 20cm (8in) round dish with clingfilm.
2 Place syrup, sugar and butter into a bowl and heat for 2–2½ min. Stir until well blended and the sugar is dissolved.
3 Stir in the remaining ingredients and place in the prepared container.
4 Cook for 4–5 min, turning every 1¼ min.
5 Leave for a few minutes to set and then mark into wedges.
6 When cool, remove from dish and serve cut into wedges.

3 × 15ml tbsp (3tbsp) golden syrup
100g (4oz) demerara sugar
100g (4oz) butter or margarine
225g (½lb) rolled oats
1 × 5ml tsp (1tsp) baking powder
½ × 5ml tsp (½tsp) salt
1 egg, beaten

Alternative conventional bake
Place mixture in a lightly greased dish or tin. Cook in a preheated oven at 180°C (350°F) Mark 4 for 30–40 min.

Peanut butter cookies *(makes about 36)*
POWER SETTING 7 (FULL OR HIGH)

100g (4oz) butter
225g (½lb) soft brown sugar
100g (4oz) peanut butter
1 egg, beaten
175g (6oz) plain flour
¼ × 5ml tsp (¼tsp) baking powder
¼ × 5ml tsp (¼tsp) salt
1 × 5ml tsp (1tsp) vanilla essence

1 Cream the butter, add the sugar and beat well until soft. Beat in the peanut butter and the egg.
2 Sift the flour, baking powder and salt. Mix into the creamed mixture and add the vanilla essence.
3 Form the mixture into small balls, allowing 2 × 5ml tsp (2tsp) mixture for each. Flatten the balls of dough with a fork dipped in sugar.
4 Place 6 at a time on a microwave baking tray or on lightly greased grease-proof paper on the cooker shelf and cook for 1¾–2½ min depending on size. Turn once halfway through.
5 Leave to cool on wire rack. Repeat with remaining mixture.

Alternative conventional bake
Place on lightly greased baking trays. Cook in a preheated oven at 200°C (400°F) Mark 6 for 15–20 min.

Almond slices *(makes about 12 slices)*
POWER SETTING 6 (ROAST OR MEDIUM/HIGH)

3 egg whites
100g (4oz) ground almonds
175g (6oz) caster sugar
50g (2oz) self-raising flour
few drops almond essence
25–50g (1–2oz) almonds, blanched and chopped

1 Lightly grease a dish approximately 15 × 15cm (6 × 6in) square or equivalent size oblong dish.
2 Whisk egg whites until stiff and holding shape, then carefully fold in the ground almonds, caster sugar, sifted flour and almond essence with a metal spoon.
3 Place the mixture into the prepared dish, smooth the top and scatter with the chopped almonds.
4 Cook on variable power setting 6 (roast or medium/high) for 5–6 min, turning every 1½ min.
5 Leave to cool for a few minutes before cutting into slices and removing to a wire rack to cool.

Alternative conventional bake
Place the mixture in a greased oven dish or tin. Cook in a preheated oven at 180°C (350°F) Mark 4 for 25–30 min.

Selection of small cakes
1 Chocolate Cup Cakes
2 Iced Cakes   3 Madeleines
4 Swiss Tartlets   5 Coconut Drops
6 Rum Truffle Cakes
7 Queen Cakes

50g (2oz) butter or margarine
50g (2oz) plain chocolate
150g (5oz) dark soft brown sugar
50g (2oz) self-raising flour
pinch salt
2 eggs, beaten
$\frac{1}{2} \times$ 5ml tsp ($\frac{1}{2}$tsp) vanilla essence
50g (2oz) walnuts, chopped
demerara sugar for sprinkling

Walnut and chocolate brownies *(makes 12–16)*
POWER SETTING 7 (FULL OR HIGH)

1 Line a 17.5cm (7in) square dish or equivalent size oblong dish.
2 Melt the butter and chocolate for about 3 min, mix well together and add the sugar.
3 Sift the flour and salt into a bowl and add the chocolate mixture, eggs, vanilla essence and walnuts. Beat until smooth and pour into the prepared container.
4 Cook for 4–5 min, turning every min.
5 Leave for 1–2 min to cool before sprinkling with demerara sugar.
6 Mark into squares and leave to cool before cutting and serving.

Alternative conventional bake
Place the mixture into a lightly greased dish or tin and cook in a preheated oven at 180°C (350°F) Mark 4 for 30–35 min.

75g (3oz) plain flour
75g (3oz) wholemeal flour
50g (2oz) ground rice
pinch salt
150g (5oz) butter
25g (1oz) caster sugar
caster sugar for dusting

Shortbread *(makes 8 wedges)*
POWER SETTING 7 (FULL OR HIGH)

1 Line a 17.5cm (7in) flan dish with clingfilm.
2 Sift the flours, rice and salt into a mixing bowl.
3 Rub in the butter finely.
4 Stir in the sugar and bring the mixture together with the palm of the hand and knead lightly.
5 Press the mixture into the prepared dish and smooth the top with a palette knife.
6 Mark into 8 and prick well with a fork.
7 Cook for 3–4 min, giving a quarter turn every min.
8 Cool slightly, sprinkle with sugar then cut into pieces. Turn out and leave to cool on a cooling rack.

Alternative conventional bake
Place mixture into a lightly greased dish or sandwich tin and cook in a preheated oven at 150°C (300°F) Mark 3 for 45–65 min.

Note: *The wholemeal flour gives a nutty texture to the shortbread but, if preferred, use all plain white flour.*

Shortbread mixture (as above)

For the topping:
50g (2oz) butter
50g (2oz) caster sugar
1 × 15ml tbsp (1tbsp) golden syrup
200g (7oz) condensed milk
75g (3oz) plain chocolate

Caramel shortbread *(makes 8 wedges)*
POWER SETTING 7 (FULL OR HIGH)

1 Follow the ingredients and method for Shortbread using all plain flour. When cooked, leave in the dish and prepare the topping.
2 Place all the ingredients except the chocolate into a bowl and heat for about 3 min. Stir until well blended and the sugar is dissolved.
3 Heat until boiling and, stirring every $\frac{1}{2}$ min, boil until thickened.
4 Leave to cool for 1 min before pouring over the shortbread base. Leave to cool and set.
5 Melt the chocolate for 2–2$\frac{1}{2}$ min and spread over the topping.
6 Mark into serving portions and leave until quite cold before cutting into wedges and removing from the dish.

Coconut drops *(makes about 24)*
POWER SETTING 7 (FULL OR HIGH)

2 eggs
100g (4oz) caster sugar
350g (¾lb) desiccated coconut
6 glacé cherries, quartered

1 Beat the eggs with a fork and then beat in the sugar. Stir in the coconut.
2 Place spoonfuls of the mixture into an egg cup, press down firmly and tip out onto the microwave cooker tray. Repeat until 12 coconut drops are spaced evenly on the tray.
3 Cook for 1¾–2¼ min, depending on the size of the egg cup shapes. Repeat with the remaining mixture.
4 Leave on wire rack to cool and top each with a quarter of glacé cherry.

Note: The contrast between the white coconut and the red cherry looks attractive, but if you prefer a browner finish, use soft brown sugar instead of the caster sugar and brown the coconut (page 149) before folding into the eggs and sugar.

Alternative conventional bake
Place the shaped drops onto lightly greased baking trays and cook in a preheated oven at 180°C (350°F) Mark 4 for 20–25 min.

Date fudge fingers *(makes 16)*
POWER SETTING 7 (FULL OR HIGH)

225g (½lb) Marie biscuits, crumbed
50g (2oz) walnuts, chopped
100g (4oz) dates, stoned and chopped
½ × 5ml tsp (½tsp) vanilla essence
2 × 5ml tsp (2tsp) cocoa powder
2 × 5ml tsp (2tsp) instant coffee powder
175g (6oz) plain chocolate
250g (9oz) condensed milk

1 Lightly grease a 20cm (8in) square or equivalent size oblong dish or tin.
2 Mix the biscuit crumbs, walnuts and dates together.
3 Place the rest of the ingredients into a bowl and melt in the microwave for 2–3 min. Stir well until blended.
4 Pour the melted mixture onto the dry ingredients and mix thoroughly.
5 Turn into the prepared container and press down well, smooth the top and mark into fingers.
6 Place in the refrigerator until set. Cut into fingers before serving.

Florentine slices *(makes about 16)*
POWER SETTING 7 (FULL OR HIGH) AND 6 (ROAST OR MEDIUM/HIGH)

75g (3oz) butter
3 × 15ml tbsp (3tbsp) golden syrup
100g (4oz) rolled oats
25g (1oz) soft brown sugar
25g (1oz) peel, finely chopped
25g (1oz) glacé cherries, finely chopped
25g (1oz) walnuts, finely chopped
100g (4oz) plain chocolate

1 Lightly grease a 20cm (8in) square dish or equivalent size oblong dish and line the base with rice paper.
2 Melt the butter and golden syrup for 1½ min. Stir until blended and stir in all the other ingredients except the chocolate.
3 Spoon the mixture into the prepared dish and press over the base.
4 Cook on variable power setting 6 (roast or medium/high) for about 6 min, turning every 2 min. Allow to cool slightly, cut into squares and place on a cooling rack until cold.
5 Melt the chocolate for 2–3 min and spread over the base of the Florentines. When nearly set, make ripples in the chocolate with the prongs of a fork.

Alternative conventional bake
Place the mixture in a lightly greased square dish or tin and line the base with rice paper. Cook in a preheated oven at 180°C (350°F) Mark 4 for 10–15 min.

Oat cookies *(makes about 18)*
POWER SETTING 7 (FULL OR HIGH) AND 6 (ROAST OR MEDIUM/HIGH)

1 Lightly grease a 17.5cm (7in) square dish or equivalent size oblong dish.
2 Melt the butter for 1½–2 min, add syrup, salt and vanilla essence, mix well together.
3 Mix the rolled oats and sugar, add to the melted mixture ensuring that it is evenly mixed.
4 Press mixture into the prepared container and cook on variable power setting 6 (roast or medium/high) for 5–6 min, giving a ¼ turn every minute. Allow to cool.
5 Melt chocolate for about 3 min and spread over the top. Sprinkle with the chopped nuts.
6 Leave to set and cut into bars.

Alternative conventional bake
Place mixture in a lightly greased square dish or tin and cook in a preheated oven at 180°C (350°F) Mark 4 for 20–30 min.

100g (4oz) butter or margarine
3 × 15ml tbsp (3tbsp) golden syrup
¼ × 5ml tsp (¼tsp) salt
1 × 5ml tsp (1tsp) vanilla essence
100g (4oz) rolled oats
100g (4oz) dark soft brown sugar
175g (6oz) plain chocolate
50g (2oz) almonds, blanched and chopped

Selection of biscuits
1 *Flapjacks* 2 *Almond Slices*
3 *Peanut Butter Cookies*
4 *Florentine Slices* 5 *Shortbread*

Richer cakes and gâteaux

2 eggs, beaten

2 × 15ml tbsp (2tbsp) black treacle

175g (6oz) dark soft brown sugar

2½ × 15ml tbsp (2½tbsp) oil

175g (6oz) self-raising flour

½ × 5ml tsp (½tsp) salt

1 × 5ml tsp (1tsp) mixed spice

150ml (¼pt) milk

450g (1lb) mixed dried fruit

50g (2oz) glacé cherries, quartered

50g (2oz) mixed chopped peel

50g (2oz) chopped nuts

Rich fruit cake (cuts into 8 or 12)
POWER SETTING 3 (STEW OR MEDIUM/LOW)

Although it is difficult to obtain good results with rich fruit cake mixtures, this recipe has been developed especially for the microwave using a low power setting

1 Lightly grease a 18.75cm (7½in) round cake dish and line the base with a circle of greaseproof paper.
2 Mix together the eggs, treacle, sugar and oil. Sift the flour, salt and mixed spice.
3 Gradually stir in the flour, salt and mixed spice alternately with the milk. Mix thoroughly.
4 Add the fruit, peel and nuts and place the mixture into the prepared container; smooth the top.
5 Cook on variable power setting 3 (stew or medium/low) for 40–50 min or until a skewer leaves the centre of the cake clean.
6 Leave for 30–40 min before turning out onto a cooling rack.

Alternative conventional bake
Place mixture in a greased and lined round cake tin and cook in a preheated oven at 150°C (300°F) Mark 2 for 2½–3 hrs.

Note: *The cake may be decorated with marzipan and glacé fruits or royal icing, in which case it is best left to mature for up to a week well wrapped in greaseproof paper and aluminium foil.*

175g (6oz) glacé cherries

350g (¾lb) sultanas

100g (4oz) plain flour

pinch salt

75g (3oz) butter

1 lemon, grated rind

75g (3oz) caster sugar

2 eggs, beaten

Rich sultana and cherry cake (cuts into 8)
POWER SETTING 5 (BAKE OR MEDIUM/HIGH)

1 Lightly grease an 18.75cm (7½in) round cake dish and line the base with a circle of greaseproof paper.
2 Wash and dry the cherries thoroughly. Cut in half and mix with the sultanas.
3 Sift the flour with the salt and add about a third to the cherries and sultanas. Toss so that the fruit is lightly coated with the flour.
4 Cream the butter, add the lemon rind and sugar and beat together until light and fluffy.
5 Add the eggs gradually, beating well after each addition.
6 Fold in the flour alternately with the fruit.
7 Place into the prepared container and smooth the top.
8 Cook on variable power setting 5 (bake or medium/high) for 12–15 min turning every 3 min, or until a skewer leaves the centre of the cake clean.
9 Leave for 20–30 min before turning out onto a cooling rack.

Alternative conventional bake
Place mixture in a lightly greased and floured round cake tin and cook in a preheated oven at 180°C (350°F) Mark 4 for 1 hr reducing to 160°C (325°F) Mark 3 for a further hour or until cooked through.

Scandinavian apple cake *(serves 6–8)*
POWER SETTING 7 (FULL OR HIGH)

1 Peel, core and slice the apples. Sprinkle the slices with lemon juice and place in a roasting or boiling bag with the caster sugar.
2 Loosely seal the top of the bag and cook for 7–10 min, turning frequently (the amount of cooking will depend on the type of cooking apple). Break down the apples with a fork if necessary.
3 Melt the butter in a bowl for 2–3 min. Stir in the breadcrumbs, demerara sugar and cinnamon, mixing well together.
4 Layer the apple and crumb mixtures in a shallow serving dish, starting and finishing with a layer of crumb mixture. Press each layer down lightly.
5 Chill in the refrigerator and before serving, decorate the top with whipped cream and grated chocolate or simply sprinkle with the chocolate.

675g (1½lb) cooking apples
few drops lemon juice
100g (4oz) caster sugar
100g (4oz) butter
175g (6oz) fresh brown breadcrumbs
100g (4oz) demerara sugar
1 × 5ml tsp (1tsp) cinnamon
150ml (¼pt) double cream, whipped, optional
25g (1oz) plain chocolate, finely grated

Brandy coffee cake
POWER SETTING 7 (FULL OR HIGH)

A rich cake to serve on its own or as a dessert course

1 Lightly grease a 20cm (8in) microwave ring mould.
2 Cream the butter, add the soft brown sugar and beat together until light and fluffy.
3 Add the eggs gradually, beating well after each addition.
4 Sift the flour and salt and fold into the creamed mixture with a metal spoon. Add the hot water and fold into the mixture.
5 Spoon the mixture into the container, smooth the top and cook for 6–7 min, turning every 1½ min.
6 Leave for 10–15 min before turning out onto a cooling rack.
7 Warm the coffee with the sugar, stir until the sugar is dissolved. Add brandy to taste.
8 When the cake is cold, return it to the ring mould and pour the coffee mixture over the cake and chill.
9 To serve, turn out and decorate with cream either spread or piped over the top and sides of the cake. Arrange the browned almonds over the top.

Alternative conventional bake
Place mixture into a lightly greased and floured ring mould or tin and cook in a preheated oven at 190°C (375°F) Mark 5 for 35–40 min.

175g (6oz) butter
175g (6oz) soft brown sugar
3 eggs, beaten
175g (6oz) self-raising flour
pinch salt
1 × 15ml tbsp (1tbsp) hot water
150–275ml (¼–½pt) strong black coffee
sugar to taste
brandy to taste
275ml (½pt) double cream, whipped
50g (2oz) almonds, browned (page 149)

Rich almond cake *(cuts into 6)*
POWER SETTING 7 (FULL OR HIGH)

This rich cake also makes a good accompaniment to fruit compôte served as a dessert course to a meal

1 Lightly grease a 17.5cm (7in) soufflé dish and line the base with a circle of greaseproof paper.
2 Cream the butter, add the sugar and beat well together until light and fluffy.
3 Add the eggs gradually, beating well after each addition.
4 Fold in the almonds, flour and essence with a metal spoon and turn mixture into the prepared container.
5 Cook for 4½–5½ min turning once halfway through.

150g (5oz) butter
175g (6oz) caster sugar
3 eggs, beaten
100g (4oz) ground almonds
50g (2oz) plain flour
few drops almond essence
caster sugar for dusting

6 Leave for 10–15 min before turning onto wire rack to cool.
7 Dust with caster sugar.

Alternative conventional bake
Place the mixture into a lightly greased and floured cake tin and cook in a preheated oven at 180°C (350°F) Mark 4 for 50–60 min.

175g (6oz) butter

175g (6oz) light soft brown sugar

3 eggs, beaten

225g (½lb) self-raising flour

40g (1½oz) glacé pineapple, finely chopped

40g (1½oz) glacé cherries, finely chopped

40g (1½oz) angelica, finely chopped

40g (1½oz) crystallised ginger, finely chopped

25g (1oz) walnuts, chopped

few drops almond essence

milk for mixing

Lemon Buttercream (page 151)

Crystallised fruit gâteau *(cuts into 8 or 12)*
POWER SETTING 7 (FULL OR HIGH)

1 Lightly grease an 18.75 (7½in) round cake dish and line the base with a circle of greaseproof paper.
2 Cream the butter, add the sugar and beat well together until light and fluffy. Add the eggs gradually, beating well after each addition.
3 Sift the flour and add about a third to the chopped fruits, tossing over well.
4 Fold in the remaining flour with the fruit, nuts and almond essence to the creamed mixture using a metal spoon; mix thoroughly.
5 Stir in just sufficient milk to give a soft dropping consistency.
6 Turn into the prepared container and cook for 7–8 min, turning every 2 min. Test with a fine skewer – it should come out clean when the cake is cooked.
7 Leave for 10–15 min before turning onto a wire rack to cool.
8 When cold, coat with lemon buttercream and pat with a palette knife to give a spiked appearance.

Alternative conventional bake
Place mixture into a lightly greased and floured cake tin and cook in a preheated oven at 180°C (350°F) Mark 4 for 1¼–1½ hrs.

Rich Fruit Cake and Christmas Pudding

225g (½lb) plain chocolate

225g (½lb) butter

2 eggs

25g (1oz) caster sugar

1–2 × 15ml tbsp (1–2tbsp) rum or brandy

100g (4oz) digestive biscuits, crumbed

100g (4oz) ground almonds

whipped cream, optional

Chocolate Caraque (page 152) or grated chocolate for sprinkling

Rum chocolate cake (serves 8)
POWER SETTING 7 (FULL OR HIGH)

This uncooked rich cake can also be served as a dessert course for a special dinner party

1 Lightly grease a 15cm (6in) loose-bottomed cake tin.
2 Break up the chocolate and melt with the butter for 3–4 min. Mix well together.
3 Whisk the eggs with the sugar until really thick and foamy. Beat in the chocolate mixture and the rum or brandy.
4 Fold in the biscuit crumbs and almonds.
5 Spoon into the prepared container, press down and smooth the top. Leave to set in the refrigerator.
6 Remove from the tin and serve piped with whipped cream and sprinkled with chocolate caraque. Alternatively, just sprinkle with grated chocolate.

100g (4oz) butter or margarine

50g (2oz) dark soft brown sugar

2 × 15ml tbsp (2tbsp) golden syrup

2 eggs, beaten

175g (6oz) self-raising flour

1 × 5ml tsp (1tsp) ground ginger

75g (3oz) crystallised ginger, finely chopped

Ginger Glacé Icing (page 150)

few pieces crystallised ginger

Ginger ring cake (cuts into 8–10)
POWER SETTING 7 (FULL OR HIGH)

1 Lightly grease a 20cm (8in) microwave ring mould.
2 Cream the butter, add the sugar and golden syrup and beat together until light and fluffy.
3 Add the eggs gradually, beating well after each addition.
4 Sift the flour and ground ginger and fold into the creamed mixture alternately with the chopped ginger, using a metal spoon.
5 Place in the prepared ring mould and cook for 5–6 min, turning every 2 min.
6 Leave for 10–15 min before turning onto a cooling rack.
7 When cold, pour the icing over the cake and allow to trickle down the sides. Decorate with crystallised ginger.

Alternative conventional bake
Place mixture into a greased and floured ring mould or tin. Cook in a preheated oven at 180°C (350°F) Mark 4 for 1–1¼ hrs.

Note: *If freezing this cake, do not ice before freezing. Finish and decorate just before serving.*

175g (6oz) butter

75g (3oz) demerara sugar

2 × 15ml tbsp (2tbsp) clear honey

3 eggs, beaten

125g (4½oz) self-raising flour

40g (1½oz) cocoa

1 × 5ml tsp (1tsp) instant coffee

4 × 15ml tbsp (4tbsp) hot water

few drops vanilla essence

Chocolate Fudge Icing (page 152)

Chocolate honey cake (cuts into 8)
POWER SETTING 7 (FULL OR HIGH)

1 Lightly grease an 18.75cm (7½in) cake dish and line the base with a circle of greaseproof paper.
2 Cream the butter, add the sugar and honey and beat well together until light and fluffy.
3 Add the eggs gradually, beating well after each addition.
4 Sift the flour and cocoa together and fold into the creamed mixture with a metal spoon.
5 Dissolve the coffee in the hot water and fold into the mixture with the vanilla essence.
6 Place mixture into the prepared container and cook for 5½–6½ min.
7 Leave until cool before turning out onto a wire rack.
8 When cold, cut in half horizontally. Sandwich the two halves together with half the fudge icing and pour the remainder over the top.

Alternative conventional bake
Divide the mixture between 2 greased and floured sandwich tins. Cook in a preheated oven at 190°C (375°F) Mark 5 for about 30 min. When cold sandwich the cakes together with half the fudge icing and pour the remainder over the top.

Note: *Do not freeze the cake with the icing. Finish and decorate just before serving.*

American fudge cake *(cuts into 8)*
POWER SETTING 7 (FULL OR HIGH)

100g (4oz) white shortening
275g (10oz) light soft brown sugar
2 eggs, beaten
225g (½lb) plain flour
½ × 5ml tsp (½tsp) baking powder
1 × 5ml tsp (1tsp) bicarbonate of soda
pinch salt
50g (2oz) cocoa
150ml (¼pt) cold water
Chocolate Fudge Icing (page 152)

1 Lightly grease an 18.75cm (7½in) cake dish and line the base with a circle of greaseproof paper.
2 Cream the fat, add the sugar and beat together until light and fluffy.
3 Add the eggs gradually, beating well after each addition.
4 Sift the flour with the baking powder, bicarbonate of soda and salt. Blend the cocoa with the water.
5 Stir the flour into the creamed mixture alternately with the cocoa and water, using a metal spoon.
6 Place the mixture into the prepared container and cook for 7–8 min, turning every 2 min. (The mixture will rise up well during cooking, but will sink back a little towards the end of the cooking).
7 Leave until cool before turning onto a wire rack.
8 When cold, cover top and sides with chocolate fudge icing.

Alternative conventional bake
Place mixture into a greased and floured cake tin and cook in a preheated oven at 180°C (350°F) Mark 4 for 40–50 min. If the top browns too much, reduce temperature to 160°C (325°F) Mark 3 until cooked through.

Note: *Do not freeze the cake with the icing. Finish and decorate just before serving.*

Raspberry millefeuille *(cuts into 8–10)*
POWER SETTING 7 (FULL OR HIGH)

225g (½lb) frozen puff pastry, thawed
275ml (½pt) double cream, whipped
450g (1lb) raspberries, washed and dried
4 × 15ml tbsp (4tbsp) redcurrant jelly
100g (4oz) almonds, browned and chopped

1 Roll out the pastry on a floured board until about 3–4mm (⅛in) thick.
2 Cut a circle measuring 22.5–25cm (9–10in) in diameter, using a large saucepan lid or dinner plate as a guide.
3 Place the pastry circle on 2 layers of kitchen paper onto the microwave shelf, cover with another piece of kitchen paper.
4 Cook for 6–7 min until well risen and firm. If necessary, turn the pastry circle over and cook for another ½ min. (The pastry may brown slightly in places, but provided it does not burn, the flavour is not altered. Any browning only has the same flavour as if it were cooked conventionally).
5 Leave to cool on a wire rack.
6 When cold, divide into 3 slices horizontally.
7 Chop half the raspberries and add to the cream. Sandwich the pastry circles together with the cream, pressing each layer down firmly.
8 Heat the redcurrant jelly for 1 min or until just melted; if too hot, leave to cool until slightly thickened.
9 Brush the top layer of the pastry with the redcurrant glaze, arrange the remaining raspberries on the top, then carefully brush again with the glaze.

10 Sprinkle a few chopped almonds over the top and press the remainder into the cream at the sides of the millefeuille. Chill before serving.

Alternative conventional bake
Place the pastry circle on a dampened baking tray and cook in a preheated oven at 220°C (425°F) Mark 7 for 10–15 min.

Variation
Use strawberries or blackberries instead of raspberries.

Note: *Do not freeze this dish.*

Black Forest gâteau
POWER SETTING 7 (FULL OR HIGH)

4 egg quantity chocolate-flavoured Genoese Sponge (page 57)

2 × 425g (15oz) cans black cherries

2 × 15ml tbsp (2tbsp) kirsch or cherry brandy

425ml (¾pt) double or whipping cream

75g (3oz) plain chocolate

Chocolate Caraque, optional (page 152)

1 Follow the ingredients and method for the Genoese Sponge substituting 25g (1oz) cocoa for 25g (1oz) flour. When cooked, allow to cool and cut in half horizontally.
2 Drain the cherries, reserving 150ml (¼pt) of the juice. Add the kirsch or cherry brandy to the reserved juice and use to moisten the cake halves. Stone the cherries.
3 Whip the cream until it is just holding its shape. Spread some over the bottom cake layer, and top with half the cherries. Place the top cake layer over the cherries.
4 Cover the sides and top of the cake with cream, reserving a little for decoration.
5 Grate the chocolate and press into the sides of the cake, reserving a little for decoration.
6 Place the cake onto its serving plate or dish and arrange the remaining cherries on the top. Pipe the remaining cream around the top edge and sprinkle with the remaining grated chocolate. Alternatively, arrange chocolate caraque over the top of the cherries and cream.

Note: *One can of cherry pie filling can be used instead of one can of the black cherries to fill the middle of the cake.*

Chocolate layer gâteau *(cuts into 8)*
POWER SETTING 7 (FULL OR HIGH)

4 egg quantity Genoese Sponge (page 57)

225g (½lb) Chocolate Buttercream (page 151)

100g (4oz) plain chocolate, grated

Chocolate Caraque, optional (page 152)

icing sugar for dusting

1 Follow the ingredients, method and cooking for Genoese Sponge.
2 When cooked and cold, cut into 3 horizontally and sandwich together with some of the buttercream.
3 Spread the remaining buttercream around the sides and over the top of the cake and dip into the grated chocolate.
4 Arrange chocolate caraque over the top of the cake and dust with sifted icing sugar; alternatively dust the sifted icing sugar over the top of the grated chocolate.

(front) *Genoese Sponge Sandwich,*
(left) *Rum Chocolate Cake,*
(right) *Brandy Coffee Cake*

4 egg quantity Genoese
Sponge (page 57)
225g (½lb) Coffee Buttercream
(page 151)
100g (4oz) almonds, flaked
and toasted
icing sugar for dusting

Coffee layer gâteau *(cuts into 8)*
POWER SETTING 7 (FULL OR HIGH)

1 Follow the ingredients, method and cooking for Genoese Sponge.
2 When cooked and cold, cut into 3 horizontally and sandwich together with some of the buttercream.
3 Spread the remaining buttercream around the sides and over the top of the cake and dip into the flaked almonds.
4 Dust the top of the cake with sifted icing sugar.

4 egg quantity Genoese
Sponge (page 57)
3 × 15ml tbsp (3tbsp)
chopped walnuts
150ml (¼pt) double cream,
whipped
Quick American Frosting
(page 151)
8 walnut halves for decoration

Frosted walnut gâteau *(cuts into 8)*
POWER SETTING 7 (FULL OR HIGH)

The basic cake is cut into 3 or 4 thin layers and is usually better made one or two days in advance

1 Follow the ingredients, method and cooking for Genoese Sponge.
2 When cooked and cold, carefully cut the cake horizontally into 3 or 4 thin circles. (Often it is easier to cut if the cake is made 1 or 2 days before and kept well wrapped or in an airtight tin).
3 Fold the chopped walnuts into the whipped cream and use to sandwich the layers together.
4 Cover the sides and top of the cake with the quick American frosting, using a palette knife to give a swirled effect. Decorate the top with 8 halves of walnut.

Frosted cherry gâteau *(cuts into 8)*

Follow the ingredients and method for the Frosted Walnut Gâteau, substituting a small bottle of maraschino cherries for the walnuts. Drain and halve the cherries and add the whipped cream. Sandwich the layers together and cover with quick American frosting, tinted pale pink with a few drops of cochineal added during the whisking. Decorate the top with small pieces of glacé cherry.

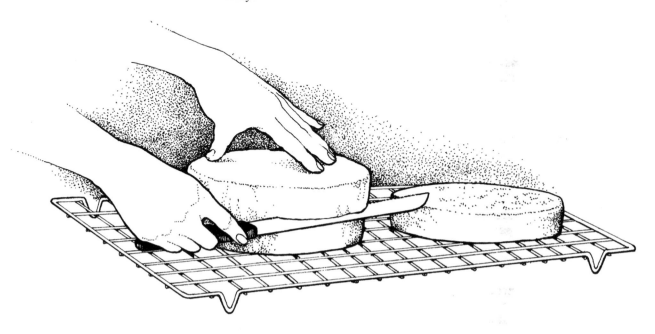

Frosted pineapple gâteau

Follow the ingredients and method for the Frosted Walnut Gâteau substituting 3 × 15ml tbsp (3tbsp) chopped, drained canned or fresh pineapple for the walnuts. Sandwich the layers together and cover with quick American frosting, tinted pale yellow with a few drops of yellow food colouring. Decorate the top with glacé or crystallised pineapple.

Note: *If freezing these cakes, freeze the basic cake on its own or in layers with the whipped cream filling. Just before serving, coat with the quick American frosting and decorate.*

...enspiegel
in Erfurt —
...Esel
...ten Psalmbuch lesen lehrte,
...Hafer zwischen die Blätter tät!

Puddings and desserts

Of all nationalities, it is probably the British who are best known for the variety and assortment of their hot dessert puddings. Whether sponge or suet, steamed or baked, all these are eminently achievable in next to no time in the microwave cooker without those traditional 'steamy days' spent in the kitchen. Although traditional pies are not successful as the filling tends to boil out before the pastry top is cooked, a selection of puddings, crumbles, flans and tarts are all here ready for you to try.

Many of the mixtures for puddings require similar techniques and methods to those given in the 'Cakes' section and I would suggest you read the introductory pages to that section as a useful guide. For pastry used in the various recipes, see the 'Pastry' section towards the end of the book.

When cooking steamed puddings in the microwave cooker they should be covered with clingfilm to keep in the moisture. However, the clingfilm should be slit with the pointed end of a knife to prevent air being trapped inside, otherwise it may cause the clingfilm to expand like a balloon. When steaming puddings conventionally, they should be covered securely with aluminium foil, greased greaseproof paper or a pudding cloth. The pudding is then placed in a steamer over a pan of gently boiling water or in a saucepan of gently boiling water with a tight fitting lid; the water level should be between a third and halfway up the basin. During the cooking period, it may be necessary to add water to maintain the level, in which case use boiling water from a kettle.

Most puddings freeze extremely well, perhaps with the exception of egg custard-based ones, and with a selection in the freezer you have an instant 'sweet trolley' available for the family. The advantage with the microwave is that individual portions can be chosen, thawed and reheated whilst the dishes from the main course are cleared.

Puddings

Chocolate pudding (serves 6–8)
POWER SETTING 7 (FULL OR HIGH)

1 Lightly grease a 1¼l (2pt) pudding basin.
2 Break up the chocolate and place in a bowl with the butter or margarine, milk, brown sugar and vanilla essence. Heat for about 2½ min then stir until blended.
3 Beat the egg yolks and stir into the chocolate mixture with the bread-crumbs.
4 Whisk the egg whites until stiff and fold into the mixture.
5 Pour into the prepared pudding basin and cover with clingfilm, slit with the pointed end of a sharp knife.
6 Cook for 6½–7½ min, turning once halfway through.
7 Leave to stand for 5 min before turning out.
8 Serve with a little chocolate sauce poured over the pudding and serve the rest of the sauce separately.

Alternative conventional bake
Cover the basin securely with greased aluminium foil. Place in a steamer over a pan of gently boiling water and steam 1½–2 hrs.

75g (3oz) plain chocolate
50g (2oz) butter or margarine
275ml (½pt) milk
75g (3oz) soft brown sugar
1 × 5ml tsp (1tsp) vanilla essence
2 eggs, separated
150g (5oz) brown breadcrumbs
For serving:
Chocolate Sauce (page 146)

Coffee Layer Gâteau

50g (2oz) self-raising flour

50g (2oz) brown breadcrumbs

1 × 5ml tsp (1tsp) mixed spice

25g (1oz) soft brown sugar

50g (2oz) shredded suet

100g (4oz) mixed dried fruit (raisins, currants, sultanas, chopped peel)

1 egg, beaten

4 × 15ml tbsp (4tbsp) milk

For serving:

Syrup Sauce (page 146)

50g (2oz) self-raising flour

50g (2oz) white breadcrumbs

25g (1oz) caster sugar

50g (2oz) shredded suet

100g (4oz) mixed glacé fruits (pineapple, cherries, crystallised ginger, angelica), chopped

1 egg, beaten

1 × 5ml tsp (1tsp) vanilla essence

4 × 15ml tbsp (4tbsp) milk

For serving:

Lemon Foamy Sauce (page 147)

225g ($\frac{1}{2}$lb) Suet Crust Pastry (page 145)

100g (4oz) jam or mincemeat

1 × 15ml tbsp (1tbsp) caster sugar

$\frac{1}{2}$ × 5ml tsp ($\frac{1}{2}$tsp) cinnamon

For serving:

Jam Sauce (page 146) and/or Custard Sauce (page 146)

College pudding (*serves 5–6*)
POWER SETTING 7 (FULL OR HIGH)

1 Lightly grease a 850ml (1$\frac{1}{2}$pt) pudding basin.
2 Sift the flour and stir in all the dry ingredients.
3 Add the egg to the milk and stir into the dry ingredients to make a soft dropping consistency. Add a little extra milk if required.
4 Turn into the prepared basin and cover with clingfilm. Slit the clingfilm with the pointed end of a sharp knife. Cook for 4$\frac{1}{2}$–5$\frac{1}{2}$ min.
5 Leave to stand for 5 min before turning out.
6 Serve hot with syrup sauce.

Alternative conventional bake
Cover the basin securely with greased aluminium foil. Place in a steamer over a pan of gently boiling water and steam for 2–2$\frac{1}{2}$ hrs.

Glacé fruit pudding (*serves 4–5*)
POWER SETTING 7 (FULL OR HIGH)

1 Lightly grease a 850ml (1$\frac{1}{2}$pt) pudding basin.
2 Sift the flour and mix in all the dry ingredients.
3 Mix the egg, vanilla essence and milk together and stir into the dry ingredients to make a soft dropping consistency. Add a little extra milk if necessary.
4 Turn into the prepared basin and cover with clingfilm. Slit the clingfilm with the pointed end of a sharp knife.
5 Cook for 4$\frac{1}{2}$–5$\frac{1}{2}$ min, turning once halfway through.
6 Leave to stand for 5 min before turning out. Serve hot with lemon foamy sauce.

Alternative conventional bake
Cover the basin securely with greased aluminium foil. Place in a steamer over a pan of gently boiling water and steam for 1$\frac{1}{2}$–2 hrs.

Roly poly pudding (*serves 6*)
POWER SETTING 7 (FULL OR HIGH)

1 On a floured surface, roll out the pastry into a square 22.5 × 22.5cm (9 × 9in) about 6mm ($\frac{1}{4}$in) thick.
2 Warm the jam or mincemeat for 30 sec and spread over the pastry leaving a border 1.25cm ($\frac{1}{2}$in) all round.
3 Roll up like a swiss roll, sealing the top and edges.
4 Place with the top edge down on a large piece of greased greaseproof paper. Roll up loosely around the pastry, allowing sufficient room for it to rise. Tie the ends with string or rubber bands and cover loosely with clingfilm.
5 Place on the microwave shelf and cook for 7$\frac{1}{2}$–8$\frac{1}{2}$ min until well risen and cooked through. Test with a fine skewer pierced through the coverings.
6 Mix the sugar and cinnamon together. Remove clingfilm and the greaseproof from the roly poly and sprinkle with the cinnamon sugar.
7 Serve hot with jam sauce and/or custard sauce.

Alternative conventional bake
Place the covered roly poly in a steamer over a pan of gently boiling water and steam for 1$\frac{1}{2}$–2 hrs.

Christmas pudding (*serves about 12*)
POWER SETTING 7 (FULL OR HIGH)

1 Lightly grease 3 × 550ml (1pt) pudding basins or 2 × 850ml (1½pt) pudding basins.
2 Sift the flour and spice into a large bowl. Add all the dry ingredients and mix well together.
3 Mix in all the other ingredients. (The mixture will improve in flavour if now left covered overnight in a cool place).
4 Divide the mixture between the 3 smaller basins or the 2 larger ones. Cover each with clingfilm and make a slit in the top with the pointed end of a sharp knife.
5 Cook each small pudding for 5 min, or each larger one for 7–9 min. In either case, allow to stand for 5–10 min before turning out.
6 Serve hot with cornflour, brandy or sherry sauce and/or rum or brandy butter.

Alternative conventional bake
Cover the basins with greased greaseproof paper, then securely with aluminium foil. Steam in a steamer over a pan of gently boiling water or boil in a saucepan with a tightly fitting lid (the water should come a third of the way up the sides of the pudding basin). Cook for 6–7 hours depending on size, and a further 2–3 hours before serving.

Note: *The puddings may be cooked and then left to mature wrapped in greaseproof paper and then in aluminium foil. On the day, they can be reheated in 2–3 min, depending on size, or in individual portions for about 1 min each.*

150g (5oz) plain flour
3 × 5ml tsp (3tsp) mixed spice
175g (6oz) breadcrumbs
225g (½lb) soft brown sugar
225g (½lb) shredded suet
575g (1¼lb) mixed dried fruit (raisins, currants, sultanas)
50g (2oz) mixed chopped peel
50g (2oz) glacé cherries, quartered
1 orange, grated rind
1 medium dessert apple, peeled and grated
4 eggs
3 × 15ml tbsp (3tbsp) black treacle
1 × 15ml tbsp (1tbsp) malt extract
2 × 15ml tbsp (2tbsp) milk
150ml (¼pt) stout

For serving:
Cornflour Sauce (page 145), Brandy or Sherry Sauce and/or Rum or Brandy Butter (page 146)

Ginger marmalade pudding (*serves 6–8*)
POWER SETTING 7 (FULL OR HIGH)

1 Lightly grease a 1¼l (2pt) pudding basin.
2 Sift the flour, baking powder and ground ginger. Stir in the breadcrumbs, suet and sugar.
3 Reserving 1½ × 15ml tbsp (1½tbsp) of the marmalade, add the rest to the dry ingredients with the eggs and add just sufficient milk to give a soft dropping consistency.
4 Place the reserved marmalade over the base of the prepared basin. Place the mixture on top and smooth the surface. Cover with clingfilm, slit with the pointed end of a sharp knife.
5 Cook for 9–10 min, turning once halfway through. Leave to stand for 5 min before turning out.
6 Serve hot with ginger marmalade sauce.

Alternative conventional bake
Cover the basin securely with greased aluminium foil and place in a steamer over a pan of gently boiling water and steam for 1¾–2¼ hrs.

Variations
If preferred, orange, lemon or lime marmalade may be used instead of ginger, in which case omit the ground ginger and replace with grated rind of an orange or lemon.

100g (4oz) plain flour
1 × 5ml tsp (1tsp) baking powder
½ × 5ml tsp (½tsp) ground ginger
100g (4oz) brown breadcrumbs
100g (4oz) shredded suet
50g (2oz) soft brown sugar
6 × 15ml tbsp (6tbsp) ginger marmalade
2 eggs, beaten
150ml (¼pt) milk, approximately

For serving:
Marmalade Sauce (page 146)

85

Syrup sponge pudding *(serves 5–6)*
POWER SETTING 7 (FULL OR HIGH)

1 Line a 850ml (1½pt) pudding basin with clingfilm.
2 Cream the butter or margarine, add the caster sugar and beat well together until light and fluffy.
3 Add the eggs gradually, beating well after each addition.
4 Sift the flour and salt and fold into the creamed mixture with a metal spoon. Add the hot water and vanilla essence or lemon juice.
5 Place the golden syrup in the bottom of the prepared basin and place the sponge mixture on top.
6 Cover with clingfilm, slit with the pointed end of a sharp knife.
7 Cook for 6–7 min. Leave to stand for 5–10 min before inverting onto a serving dish or plate.
8 Serve with extra warmed syrup and custard sauce.

Alternative conventional bake
Cover the basin securely with greased aluminium foil. Place in a steamer over a pan of gently boiling water and steam for 1–1¼ hrs.

Variations
Jam – Replace the syrup with the same quantity of jam.
Raisin – Add 3 × 15ml tbsp (3tbsp) raisins with the flour.

Syrup Sponge Pudding with Jam
Sponge Pudding ready to be cooked

100g (4oz) butter or margarine
100g (4oz) caster sugar
2 eggs, beaten
100g (4oz) self-raising flour
pinch salt
1–2 × 15ml tbsp (1–2tbsp) hot water
few drops vanilla essence or lemon juice
3 × 15ml tbsp (3tbsp) golden syrup
For serving:
Custard Sauce (page 146)

Apple and honey pudding *(serves 6–8)*
POWER SETTING 7 (FULL OR HIGH)

1 Lightly grease a 1¼l (2pt) pudding basin.
2 Cream the butter or margarine, add the caster sugar and beat well together until light and fluffy.
3 Add the eggs gradually, beating well after each addition. Sift the flour and salt and fold into the creamed mixture with a metal spoon.
4 Sprinkle the prepared pudding basin with the soft brown sugar. Mix the chopped apples, nutmeg and honey, place in the basin and cover with the creamed mixture.
5 Cover with clingfilm, slit with the pointed end of a sharp knife. Cook for 7–8 min, turning once halfway through.
6 Leave for 5 min before turning out. Serve with warmed honey and custard.

Alternative conventional bake
Cover the basin securely with greased aluminium foil and place in a steamer over a pan of gently boiling water and steam for 1½–2 hrs.

100g (4oz) butter or margarine
100g (4oz) caster sugar
2 eggs, beaten
100g (4oz) self-raising flour
pinch salt
50g (2oz) soft brown sugar
2 medium dessert apples, peeled, cored and chopped
pinch grated nutmeg
3 × 15ml tbsp (3tbsp) clear honey
For serving:
warmed honey and Custard Sauce (page 146)

Three fruit pudding *(serves 6–8)*
POWER SETTING 7 (FULL OR HIGH)

1 Lightly grease a 1¼l (2pt) pudding basin.
2 Roll out two-thirds of the pastry on a floured surface and line the pudding basin.
3 Layer the fruits and sugar into the lined basin. Roll out the remaining pastry to fit the top of the pudding, dampen and seal the edges.
4 Cover the top of the basin very tightly with clingfilm.
5 Turn the basin upside down onto the microwave oven shelf and cook for 5

225g (½lb) Suet Crust Pastry (page 145)
For the filling:
450g (1lb) cooking apples, peeled, cored and chopped
225g (½lb) raspberries
225g (½lb) blackberries
100g (4oz) caster sugar
For serving:
cream

87

min. Turn the pudding the right way up and cook for a further 5 min. Remove the clingfilm and cook for another 2–3 min.
6 Allow to stand for 10–15 min before turning out of the basin.
7 Serve hot with cream.

Alternative conventional bake
Cover the basin with greased greaseproof paper and then securely with aluminium foil. Place in a steamer over a pan of gently boiling water and steam for 2½–3 hrs.

Bread and butter pudding (*serves 4*)
POWER SETTING 7 (FULL OR HIGH)

6 slices white or brown bread
75g (3oz) butter
50g (2oz) sultanas or currants
3 eggs, beaten
40g (1½oz) caster sugar
425ml (¾pt) milk
few drops vanilla essence
grated nutmeg for sprinkling, optional

1 Lightly butter a 1¼l (2pt) pie dish. Remove the crusts from the bread; spread the slices with butter and cut in half diagonally.
2 Arrange the bread in layers in the prepared dish, sprinkling each layer with the sultanas or currants.
3 Beat the eggs with the sugar. Warm the milk and vanilla essence for 1 min and add the eggs and sugar, beating well.
4 Pour the custard over the bread. Stand the pie dish in a shallow water bath in the microwave oven. (The size of the water bath and the depth of water will affect the cooking times slightly.)
5 Cook for 5 min, allow to stand for 5 min, cook for a further 5 min or until custard sets in the centre.
6 Sprinkle with grated nutmeg or crisp the top of the pudding under a hot grill before serving.

Alternative conventional bake
Cook in a preheated oven at 180°C (350°F) Mark 4 for about 1 hour.

Apple bread pudding (*cuts into 8 wedges*)
POWER SETTING 7 (FULL OR HIGH) AND 4 (DEFROST OR MEDIUM)

225g (½lb) bread
275ml (8fl oz) milk
50g (2oz) butter or margarine
50g (2oz) demerara sugar
2 × 5ml tsp (2tsp) mixed spice
1 egg, beaten
50g (2oz) mixed chopped peel
175g (6oz) mixed dried fruit (sultanas, raisins, currants, glacé cherries)
1 medium cooking apple
few drops lemon juice
demerara sugar for sprinkling

1 Lightly grease a 20cm (8in) flan dish.
2 Break the bread into small pieces and place in a bowl. Soak with milk, break down the bread with a fork. Beat thoroughly until smooth.
3 Melt the butter or margarine for 1½ min; add to the bread with the sugar, spice, egg, peel and fruit. Mix together thoroughly.
4 Turn the mixture into the prepared dish and cook on setting 4 (defrost or medium) for 10 min. Leave to stand for 5 min.
5 Peel, core and slice the apple and arrange over the top of the pudding. Sprinkle the apple with a few drops of lemon juice.
6 Cook for a further 10 min on setting 4 (defrost or medium).
7 Serve hot or cold sprinkled with demerara sugar.

Alternative conventional bake
Cook in a preheated oven at 180°C (350°F) Mark 4 for 45 min. Add the apple topping and cook for a further 20–25 min.

Castle puddings (serves 6)
POWER SETTING 7 (FULL OR HIGH)

1 Lightly grease a microwave muffin pan and divide half the jam between the 6 moulds.
2 Cream the butter or margarine, add the sugar and beat well together until light and fluffy.
3 Beat in the vanilla essence, and add the eggs gradually, beating well after each addition.
4 Fold in the sifted flour with a metal spoon and then fold in the hot water.
5 Divide half the mixture between the moulds, filling no more than two-thirds full.
6 Cook for $2\frac{1}{2}$ min, turning once halfway through.
7 Leave for a few minutes before turning out.
8 Repeat with the remaining jam and mixture.
9 Serve hot with jam sauce and custard sauce.

Alternative conventional bake
Divide the mixture between 6–8 greased dariole moulds and bake in a preheated oven at 180°C (350°F) Mark 4 for 25 min. Alternatively place the moulds in a steamer over a pan of gently boiling water and steam for 40–50 min.

100g (4oz) blackcurrant or raspberry jam
100g (4oz) butter or margarine
100g (4oz) caster sugar
1 × 5ml tsp (1tsp) vanilla essence
2 eggs, beaten
100g (4oz) self-raising flour
1 × 15ml tbsp (1tbsp) hot water
For serving:
Blackcurrant or Raspberry Jam Sauce (page 146) and Custard Sauce (page 146)

Eve's pudding (serves 6–8)
POWER SETTING 6 (ROAST OR MEDIUM/HIGH)

1 Lightly grease a 20cm (8in) soufflé dish or cake dish.
2 Peel, core and slice the apples and layer in the dish with the demerara sugar and lemon rind.
3 Cream the butter, add the caster sugar and beat well together until light and fluffy.
4 Beat in the vanilla essence and the eggs gradually, beating well after each addition.
5 Fold in the flour with a metal spoon using enough milk to give a soft consistency; spoon mixture carefully over the apples. Smooth the top.
6 Cook on variable power setting 6 (roast or medium/high) for about 12 min turning once halfway through. Test with a fine skewer which should come out clean when the sponge is cooked.
7 Sprinkle the top of the sponge heavily with demerara sugar, glaze and brown the top under a hot conventional grill.
8 Serve with cream or custard sauce.

Alternative conventional bake
Cook in a preheated oven at 180°C (350°F) Mark 4 for 35–40 min. Dredge with demerara sugar.

450g (1lb) cooking apples
75g (3oz) demerara sugar
1 lemon, grated rind
100g (4oz) butter or margarine
100g (4oz) caster sugar
1 × 5ml tsp (1tsp) vanilla essence
2 eggs, beaten
100g (4oz) self-raising flour
milk for mixing
demerara sugar for sprinkling
For serving:
cream or Custard Sauce (page 146)

175g (6oz) walnuts
100g (4oz) shredded suet
100g (4oz) brown breadcrumbs
25g (1oz) wholemeal flour
4 × 15ml tbsp (4tbsp) apricot jam
2 eggs, beaten
4 × 15ml tbsp (4tbsp) milk
For serving:
Apricot Jam Sauce (page 146)

Apricot and Walnut Pudding with Apricot Jam Sauce

Apricot and walnut pudding (*serves 5–6*)
POWER SETTING 7 (FULL OR HIGH)

1 Lightly grease a 850ml (1½pt) pudding basin.
2 Reserve 7 walnut halves and chop the rest coarsely.
3 Add the suet, breadcrumbs and flour to the chopped walnuts. Mix in the jam, eggs and milk.
4 Arrange the reserved walnut halves in the base of the prepared basin and carefully spoon the mixture over the top. Smooth the surface.
5 Cover with clingfilm, slit with the pointed end of a sharp knife.
6 Cook for 7–8 min, turning once halfway through.
7 Leave to stand for 5 min before turning out.
8 Serve with some apricot jam sauce poured over the pudding and hand the rest separately.

Alternative conventional bake
Cover the basin securely with greased aluminium foil and place in a steamer over a pan of gently boiling water and steam for 1½–2 hrs.

Note: *Almonds may be used instead of walnuts if preferred.*

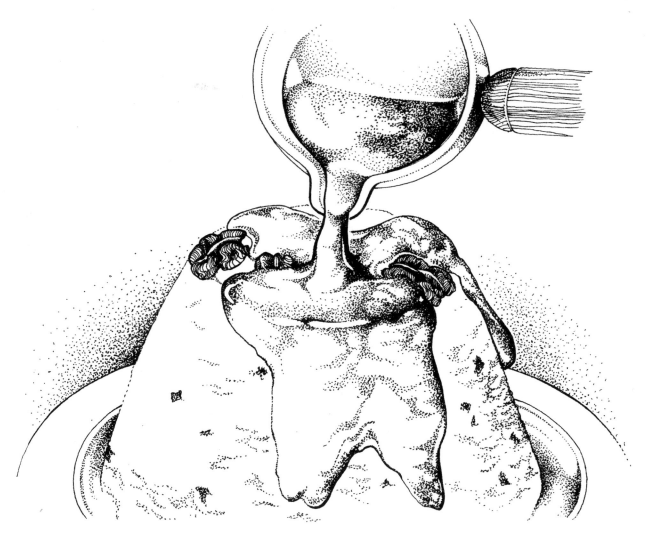

50g (2oz) butter

50g (2oz) soft brown sugar

16 apricot halves, cooked or canned

16 large prunes, cooked or canned

225g ($\frac{1}{2}$lb) self-raising flour

100g (4oz) butter or margarine

100g (4oz) caster sugar

1 lemon, grated rind

2 eggs, beaten

milk for mixing

For serving:

cream

Chequerboard upside down pudding *(serves 8–10)*
POWER SETTING 7 (FULL OR HIGH)

1 Place the butter in the bottom of a square dish measuring 20 × 20cm (8 × 8in) or equivalent size oblong dish.
2 Melt the butter for 1$\frac{1}{2}$ min and sprinkle with the soft brown sugar.
3 Arrange the apricot halves (cut side up) and the prunes in the base of the dish, alternating the fruits to give a chequerboard design.
4 Sift the flour, rub in the butter or margarine finely, stir in the sugar and the grated lemon rind.
5 Add the eggs and sufficient milk to make a soft dropping consistency. Mix well together.
6 Spoon the mixture carefully over the fruit in the dish and smooth the top.
7 Cook for 9–10 min, giving a quarter turn every 2 min. Test the centre with a skewer.
8 Serve hot or cold with cream.

Alternative conventional bake
If a metal cake tin is used, melt the butter in a dish in the microwave and pour it into the tin. Sprinkle with the soft brown sugar. Continue as above, placing the dish into a preheated oven at 180°C (350°F) Mark 4 and cook for 1–1$\frac{1}{4}$ hrs.

175g (6oz) self-raising flour

$\frac{1}{2}$ × 5ml tsp ($\frac{1}{2}$tsp) cinnamon

$\frac{1}{2}$ × 5ml tsp ($\frac{1}{2}$tsp) ground ginger

$\frac{1}{2}$ × 5ml tsp ($\frac{1}{2}$tsp) mixed spice

$\frac{1}{4}$ × 5ml tsp ($\frac{1}{4}$tsp) bicarbonate of soda

$\frac{1}{4}$ × 5ml tsp ($\frac{1}{4}$tsp) cream of tartar

50g (2oz) soft brown sugar

75g (3oz) shredded suet

175g (6oz) mixed dried fruit (currants, sultanas and stoned raisins)

$\frac{1}{2}$ apple, peeled, cored and grated

1$\frac{1}{2}$ × 15ml tbsp (1$\frac{1}{2}$tbsp) black treacle

1 egg, beaten

milk for mixing

caster sugar for sprinkling

For serving:

Rum or Brandy Butter (page 146)

Cloutie dumpling *(serves 4–6)*
POWER SETTING 7 (FULL OR HIGH)

1 Sift the flour, spices, bicarbonate of soda and cream of tartar into a bowl.
2 Add the sugar, suet and fruits, mixing well together.
3 Mix the black treacle with the egg and stir into the dry ingredients with sufficient milk to form a soft scone-type dough.
4 Knead lightly and form into a ball and place on a lightly floured, clean cloth; tie up with string or a rubber band, allowing sufficient room for the dumpling to swell.
5 Place inside a large boiling or roasting bag with about 75ml ($\frac{1}{8}$pt) of water. Seal the top loosely.
6 Cook for 5$\frac{1}{2}$–6$\frac{1}{2}$ min.
7 Remove the dumpling from the bag, open the cloth and dab away any moisture with absorbent kitchen paper. If necessary place the dumpling in the microwave and cook for a further 1 min to dry off the outside of the dumpling.
8 Sprinkle heavily with caster sugar and serve hot in slices with rum or brandy butter.

Alternative conventional bake
Place the dumpling in the cloth and tie up allowing sufficient room for the dumpling to swell. Plunge into a large pan of boiling water and boil steadily for 2–2$\frac{1}{2}$ hrs. Remove from the cloth and place in a hot dish in a moderate oven for 10 min to dry the outside. Sprinkle with caster sugar and serve hot in slices with rum or brandy butter.

Summer pudding *(serves 6)*
POWER SETTING 7 (FULL OR HIGH)

An 'uncooked' pudding – delicious when served with whipped cream

1 Pick over and wash the fruits, removing stones from cherries if used.
2 Place the fruit in a large bowl with the sugar, cover with a lid or clingfilm. Alternatively place the fruit and sugar in a boiling or roasting bag.
3 Cook for about 5 min, gently shaking or turning 2–3 times throughout to stir the contents without breaking the fruit. Leave to cool slightly; drain off and reserve some of the juice.
4 Line a 850ml (1½pt) pudding basin with the bread, starting off by cutting to fit the base, then lining the sides. Cut the slices so that the bread fits closely together. Reserve some bread for the top.
5 Spoon the fruit into basin and cover with the remaining bread.
6 Place a plate that fits inside the top of the basin over the pudding and press down with a weight. Chill for about 8 hours or overnight.
7 Remove the weight and plate and unmould the pudding onto the serving plate or dish.
8 Use the reserved juice to coat any parts of the bread which have not been soaked by the fruit juice during the chilling.
9 Serve with whipped cream.

675g (1½lb) mixed soft fruits (blackcurrants, redcurrants, raspberries, blackberries, strawberries, cherries)
100g (4oz) caster sugar
6–8 slices stale bread
For serving:
whipped double cream

Flans and desserts

Apple flan (serves 6–8)
POWER SETTING 7 (FULL OR HIGH)

1 Roll out the pastry, line a 20cm (8in) flan dish and bake blind (page 142). Reserve the trimmings.
2 Place the apples, sugar, lemon rind, butter or margarine and cinnamon or cloves into a large bowl or dish, cover and cook for 6–8 min until tender, turning or shaking the fruit once or twice. Drain off some of the juice.
3 Mash the apples down with a fork or purée in a blender and pour into the baked flan case; smooth the top.
4 Roll out the trimmings from the pastry and cut into thin strips. Lay the strips of pastry over the filling in a lattice style.
5 Cook for 3–4 min, rest for 3 min. Turn the dish and cook for a further 2–3 min until pastry lattice is cooked.
6 Leave to stand for a few minutes then sprinkle with demerara sugar before serving.

Alternative conventional bake
It is not necessary to cook the pastry case first. Cook the complete dish in a preheated oven at 190°C (375°F) Mark 5 for 35–40 min.

Variation
1–2 × 15ml tbsp (1–2tbsp) sultanas or currants may be added to the apples instead of cinnamon or cloves.

225g (½lb) Rich Shortcrust Pastry (page 144)
675g (1½lb) cooking apples, peeled, cored and sliced
75–100g (3–4oz) sugar
1 lemon, grated rind
25g (1oz) butter or margarine
ground cinnamon or cloves to taste, optional
demerara sugar for sprinkling

Mincemeat and orange flan (serves 6–8)
POWER SETTING 7 (FULL OR HIGH)

1 Place the cooked flan case on a large serving plate or in its flan dish.
2 Place the mincemeat, orange rind and juice, almonds and liqueur into a bowl, mix well together and cook for 4–5 min, stirring every minute. Allow to cool for a few minutes before spreading in the base of the flan case.
3 Peel the oranges, slice into thin rounds and arrange over the top of the mincemeat.
4 Brush with warmed apricot glaze and serve cold with cream.

1 × 20cm (8in) baked flan case using Rich Shortcrust Pastry (page 144)
450g (1lb) mincemeat
1 orange, grated rind and juice
50g (2oz) almonds, blanched and chopped
2 × 15ml tbsp (2tbsp) orange liqueur, grand marnier or cointreau
2 seedless oranges
4 × 15ml tbsp (4tbsp) Apricot Glaze (page 149)
For serving:
cream

Summer Pudding

95

1 × 20cm (8in) baked flan
case using Rich Shortcrust
Pastry (page 144)

1 × 15ml tbsp (1tbsp) custard
powder

2 × 5ml tsp (2tsp) caster
sugar

150ml (¼pt) milk

150ml (¼pt) double cream,
whipped

100g (4oz) Praline, crushed
(page 149)

2 × 450g (1lb) cans black
cherries

2 × 5ml tsp (2tsp) arrowroot

4 × 15ml tbsp (4tbsp)
redcurrant jelly

For serving:

whipped cream

Cherry and praline flan *(serves 6–8)*
POWER SETTING 7 (FULL OR HIGH)

1 Place the flan case on a large serving plate or in its flan dish.
2 Make a custard with the custard powder, caster sugar and milk, cook for
  2–3 min, stirring every minute until thick. Beat well then leave to cool.
3 When cold, whisk the custard and fold in the whipped cream and praline.
  Place the mixture in the bottom of the flan case and smooth the top.
4 Drain the cherries, reserving 150ml (¼pt) of the juice and blend with the
  arrowroot.
5 Melt the redcurrant jelly for about 1 min and add to the cherry juice and
  arrowroot. Stir well then heat for 2–3 min until thick, stirring frequently.
6 Stone the cherries if required and arrange over the praline cream. Glaze
  with the thickened juice and leave to cool and set.
7 Serve cold with whipped cream.

Variation
Substitute finely chopped hazelnuts for the crushed praline.

Note: *Do not freeze this dish.*

75g (3oz) butter

175g (6oz) digestive biscuits,
crumbed

2 × 5ml tsp (2tsp) caster
sugar

450g (1lb) cream cheese

75g (3oz) caster sugar

2 eggs, beaten

1 lemon, grated rind

½ packet lemon table jelly

Lemon cheesecake *(serves 8)*
POWER SETTING 7 (FULL OR HIGH)

1 Melt the butter in a 20cm (8in) flan dish. Toss in the biscuit crumbs and
  2 × 5ml tsp (2tsp) caster sugar. Mix well and press evenly against the base
  and sides of the dish using a metal spoon.
2 Cream the cheese, add the sugar and beat well together until soft. Add the
  eggs gradually, beating well after each addition. Finally beat in the lemon
  rind.
3 Pour the filling onto the biscuit base, smooth the top and cook for 10–12
  min, giving the dish a quarter turn every 3 min.
4 Leave to cool.
5 Break the jelly into cubes into a bowl, add 1 × 15ml tbsp (1tbsp) water and
  melt in the microwave for 15 sec. Make up to 275ml (½pt) with water. Stir
  well and, when completely blended, pour over the top of the cheesecake.
  Chill until the jelly is set.

Variation
Substitute 1 × 5ml tsp (1tsp) vanilla essence for the lemon rind and when
cold top with a fruit pie filling.

Note: *Do not freeze the lemon cheesecake with the jelly topping. Decorate and
finish before serving.*

Cherry and Praline Flan

1 × 20cm (8in) baked flan
case using Almond Pastry
(page 145)

450g (1lb) can apricots

2–3 × 15ml tbsp (2–3tbsp)
apricot jam

50g (2oz) ground almonds

275ml (½pt) double cream,
whipped

few drops almond essence

caster sugar to taste, optional

10 almonds, blanched and
split

Apricot and almond flan (serves 6–8)
POWER SETTING 7 (FULL OR HIGH)

1 Place the cooked flan case on a large serving plate or in its flan dish.
2 Drain the apricots and reserve half the syrup. Sieve the jam and blend with the apricot syrup. Boil in the microwave for 2–3 min until thickened. It should be thick enough to coat the back of a wooden spoon.
3 Fold the ground almonds into the double cream, add the almond essence and sugar to taste.
4 Spread the cream filling in the base of the pastry case. Arrange the apricots and almonds on the top and brush with the apricot glaze.
5 Serve chilled with cream.

450g (1lb) rhubarb

2–3 × 15ml tbsp (2–3tbsp)
golden syrup

175g (6oz) butter

350g (¾lb) ginger biscuits,
crumbed

1 × 15ml tbsp (1tbsp) custard
powder

1 × 5ml tsp (1tsp) ground
ginger

2 × 5ml tsp (2tsp) caster
sugar

150ml (¼pt) milk

150ml (¼pt) soured cream

For decoration:

whipped cream

Creamy rhubarb and ginger flan (serves 6–8)
POWER SETTING 7 (FULL OR HIGH)

1 Wash and trim the rhubarb and cut into 2.5cm (1in) lengths. Place with the syrup in a covered casserole, roasting or boiling bag and cook for 5–6 min until tender.
2 Melt the butter for 2–3 min, stir in the biscuit crumbs. Mix well together and press over the base and around the sides of a 20–22.5cm (8–9in) flan dish.
3 Blend the custard powder, ginger and caster sugar with the milk and cook for 2–3 min until thick, stirring every minute. When cool beat in the soured cream.
4 Drain off some of the juice from the rhubarb and combine rhubarb with the custard and cream. The mixture may be blended in a liquidiser or sieved if preferred.
5 Pour into the biscuit base and leave until cold and set. Chill before serving and pipe with whipped cream.

Note: *Do not freeze this dish.*

1 × 20cm (8in) baked flan
case using Rich Shortcrust
Pastry (page 144)

175g (6oz) cream cheese

50g (2oz) caster sugar

3 × 15ml tbsp (3tbsp) double
or soured cream

450g (1lb) strawberries

2 × 15ml tbsp (2tbsp)
redcurrant jelly

Strawberry cream flan (serves 6–8)
POWER SETTING 7 (FULL OR HIGH)

1 Place the cooked flan case on a large serving plate or in its flan dish.
2 Cream the cheese with the sugar, beating well together until light and fluffy. Beat in the cream.
3 Wash and dry the strawberries, heat the redcurrant jelly for ½–1 min until melted.
4 Spread the cream cheese mixture in the base of the flan case. Arrange the strawberries over the top and brush with the warm glaze.
5 Serve when cooled and set.

Note: *Do not freeze the flan with the strawberries. Finish and decorate just before serving.*

Cream treacle tart *(serves 6–8)*

POWER SETTING 7 (FULL OR HIGH) AND 4 (DEFROST OR MEDIUM)

1 Place the flan case on a large serving plate or in its flan dish.
2 Place the syrup, lemon rind, juice and butter in a bowl and warm for 2–3 min. Stir until blended together.
3 Beat the eggs and single cream and add the syrup, beating well.
4 Cook on setting 4 (defrost or medium) for 7–8 min, beating well with a fork every 1½ min, until thickened.
5 Pour the mixture into the flan case and leave to set when the filling will have a soft jelly-like consistency.
6 Pipe some whipped cream around the edge of the tart before serving and serve the rest separately.

Alternative conventional bake
There is no need to pre-bake the flan case. Pour the syrup mixture into the raw pastry case and cook in a preheated oven at 180°C (350°F) Mark 4 for 45–50 min.

1 × 20cm (8in) baked flan case using Rich Shortcrust Pastry (page 144)
350g (¾lb) golden syrup
½ lemon, grated rind
1 × 5ml tsp (1tsp) lemon juice
25g (1oz) butter
3 × 15ml tbsp (3tbsp) single cream
3 eggs, beaten
For serving:
whipped cream

Linzer torte *(serves 6)*

POWER SETTING 7 (FULL OR HIGH)

1 Prepare the Almond Pastry, roll out on a lightly floured surface and line a 20 cm (8in) flan dish. Reserve the trimmings. Chill the flan case for about 20 min in the refrigerator.
2 Bake the flan case blind (page 142).
3 Fill the flan case with the raspberries and sugar. Roll out the reserved pastry, cut into strips and make lattice design across the top of the flan.
4 Cook the flan for 7–8 min or until the lattice is cooked through. Allow to cool.
5 Warm the redcurrant jelly for 15–30 sec and brush over the lattice to make a thick glaze.
6 Serve cold with whipped cream.

Alternative conventional bake
Bake the flan case blind conventionally (page 142). Cook the flan, filled and topped with the lattice, in a preheated oven at 190°C (375°F) Mark 5 for 25–30 min. Finish as above.

225g (½lb) Almond Pastry (page 145)
450g (1lb) raspberries, fresh or frozen, thawed
75–100g (3–4oz) caster sugar
2 × 15ml tbsp (2tbsp) redcurrant jelly
For serving:
whipped cream

40g (1½oz) strawberry
flavoured blancmange powder

175g (6oz) plain flour

1 × 5ml tsp (1tsp) cream of
tartar

½ × 5ml tsp (½tsp) bicarbonate
of soda

pinch of salt

50g (2oz) butter or margarine

50g (2oz) caster sugar

1 egg, beaten

milk for mixing

For serving:

225g (½lb) strawberries

275ml (½pt) double cream

caster sugar to taste

butter for spreading

Strawberry shortcake *(serves 6–8)*
POWER SETTING 7 (FULL OR HIGH)

1 Line a 15–17.5cm (6–7in) flan dish with clingfilm.
2 Sift together the blancmange powder, flour, raising agents and salt. Rub in the butter or margarine finely, stir in the sugar.
3 Add the eggs and sufficient milk to make a soft manageable dough. Knead lightly and roll out on a floured surface into a circle to fit the flan dish.
4 Place the dough into the prepared dish and cook for about 6 min turning once halfway through.
5 Leave for 5–10 min before removing onto a wire rack to cool.
6 Hull, wash and dry the strawberries. Reserving a few whole ones for decoration, cut the rest into slices.
7 Whip the double cream and stir in the caster sugar to taste.
8 Cut the cold shortcake into half horizontally. Spread the bottom half with a little softened butter, and then the whipped cream, piling it up in the centre and reserving some for piping.
9 Place the sliced strawberries on the cream and top with remaining short-cake layer and cut into wedges.
10 Pipe the remaining cream on the top and decorate with the whole strawberries.

Alternative conventional bake
Place the dough into a greased and floured flan dish or sandwich tin. Bake in a preheated oven at 220°C (425°F) Mark 7 for 20–25 min.

Variation
Any fruit and matching flavour blancmange powder can be used.

6 slices white bread

3 × 15ml tbsp (3tbsp) sherry

2 × 5ml tsp (2tsp) caster
sugar

2 egg yolks, beaten

2 × 15ml tbsp (2tbsp) milk

50g (2oz) butter, melted

2 × 15ml tbsp (2tbsp) soft
brown sugar

2 × 5ml tsp (2tsp) cinnamon

For serving:

Jam Sauce (page 146)

Poor knights of Windsor *(serves 6)*
POWER SETTING 7 (FULL OR HIGH)

1 Cut the slices of bread in half diagonally and soak in the sherry mixed with the caster sugar.
2 Beat the egg yolks together with the milk and brush over the bread slices.
3 Preheat a browning dish for 7–8 min, add half the butter and cook 6 halves of the bread at a time for 1 min each side until golden brown.
4 Preheat the browning dish for 3–4 min and cook the remaining bread slices with the rest of the butter.
5 Mix the caster sugar and cinnamon and sprinkle over the hot bread. Serve with jam sauce.

Alternative conventional bake
Fry the slices of bread in a frying pan.

Strawberry Shortcake

50g (2oz) butter
225g (½lb) cream cheese
100g (4oz) caster sugar
2 eggs
50g (2oz) semolina
50g (2oz) ground almonds
½ lemon, grated rind and juice
50g (2oz) raisins
few drops almond essence
For serving:
whipped cream
chopped browned almonds

Almond pudding *(serves 4–5)*
POWER SETTING 6 (ROAST OR MEDIUM/HIGH)

1 Lightly grease a 17.5cm (7in) soufflé dish and line the base with a circle of greaseproof paper.
2 Cream the butter and cream cheese, add the caster sugar and beat well together until light and fluffy.
3 Separate the eggs and beat the yolks into the creamed mixture. Stir in the semolina, ground almonds, lemon rind, raisins and almond essence.
4 Whisk the egg whites until stiff and fold into the mixture. Pour the mixture into the prepared container.
5 Cook on variable power setting 6 (roast or medium/high) for 8–9 min until firm to touch, turning every 2 min.
6 Leave to cool for 15–20 min before turning out of dish.
7 When cold, pipe with whipped cream and sprinkle with almonds.

Alternative conventional bake
Cook in a preheated oven at 180°C (350°F) Mark 4 for 45–50 min until firm.

50g (2oz) butter
25g (1oz) caster sugar
2 × 15ml tbsp (2tbsp) ground
Praline (page 149)
rum to taste
8–10 Pancakes, cooked (page 114)
For serving:
cream

Praline and rum pancakes *(makes 8–10)*
POWER SETTING 7 (FULL OR HIGH)

1 Cream the butter, add the sugar and beat well together until light and fluffy. Mix in the praline and flavour to taste with the rum.
2 Divide the mixture between the pancakes and either roll up or fold each one into 4.
3 Place in their serving dish, cover with clingfilm and heat for 2 min, allow to stand for 2 min, then heat for a further 1–2 min or until just warmed through.
4 Serve hot with cream.

Alternative conventional bake
Place pancakes in an ovenware serving dish, cover with aluminium foil and heat through in a preheated oven at 180°C (350°F) Mark 4 for 15–20 min.

Apple pancakes

Cook 2 medium dessert apples, peeled and sliced with ¼ × 5ml tsp (¼tsp) cinnamon, 25g (1oz) brown sugar and 25g (1oz) butter for 3–4 min until soft. Fill the pancakes with 1–2 tbsp of the apple mixture, roll up and brush well with melted butter. Heat through as above and serve hot sprinkled with cinnamon and sugar.

Fresh berry pancakes

Fill hot pancakes with crushed raspberries, strawberries or blackberries mixed with whipped cream. Heat through for 1–2 min and serve garnished with whole berries.

Quick cherry strudel (*serves 6–8*)
POWER SETTING 7 (FULL OR HIGH)

Thinly rolled puff pastry makes a good substitute for strudel paste when in a hurry

1 Preheat a browning dish for 5–6 min, add the butter or margarine and, when melted, toss the breadcrumbs in the butter and cook until lightly browned for about 2 min.
2 Roll out the pastry very thinly into a large rectangle on a lightly floured surface. Spread with the melted butter.
3 Scatter the breadcrumbs over the butter then scatter on the halved cherries.
4 Mix the sugar and cinnamon and sprinkle over the cherries; sprinkle with the grated lemon rind.
5 Fold over the edges of the pastry, roll up, cook and finish as for Apple Strudel (page 105).

Alternative conventional bake
Sauté the breadcrumbs in the butter or margarine in a frying pan. Cook on a baking tray in a preheated oven at 180°C (350°F) Mark 4 for 50–60 min.

50g (2oz) butter or margarine
75g (3oz) white breadcrumbs
175g (6oz) frozen puff pastry, thawed
25g (1oz) butter, melted
450g (1lb) cherries, stoned and halved
1 × 15ml tbsp (1tbsp) soft brown sugar
1 × 5ml tsp (1tsp) cinnamon
½ lemon, grated rind
icing sugar for dredging

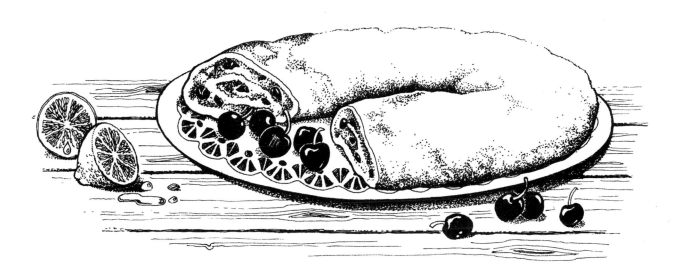

Cream cheese strudel (*serves 6–8*)
POWER SETTING 7 (FULL OR HIGH)

1 Prepare the strudel paste.
2 Place the cheese and butter into a bowl and cream together. Beat in the sugar, egg and vanilla essence.
3 Place the lemon juice and sultanas in a bowl and add sufficient water to just cover the sultanas. Cook for 2 min and leave to stand.
4 Roll out the paste as for Apple Strudel (page 105) and brush the paste with the oil.
5 Drain the sultanas and add to the cheese mixture with the lemon rind. Mix well then spread over the paste, sprinkle with the breadcrumbs.
6 Fold over the edges, roll up, cook and finish as for Apple Strudel.

100g (4oz) Strudel Paste (page 145)
125g (5oz) cream cheese
40g (1½oz) butter
25g (1oz) caster sugar
½ egg, beaten
few drops vanilla essence
1 lemon, juice and grated rind
40g (1½oz) sultanas
1 × 15ml tbsp (1tbsp) oil
25g (1oz) fresh brown breadcrumbs
icing sugar for dredging

103

Apple strudel *(serves 6–8)*
POWER SETTING 7 (FULL OR HIGH)

1 Prepare the strudel paste.
2 Melt the butter in a bowl for ½ min and stir in the breadcrumbs. In a separate bowl mix the lemon rind with the apples.
3 Roll out the strudel paste on a lightly floured, clean teatowel, pulling and stretching the paste carefully to give a large thin rectangle. You should be able to just see the pattern on the teatowel through the rolled-out pastry when it is thin enough.
4 Brush the paste with the oil and spread with the jam. Sprinkle with the breadcrumbs, the apple and lemon mixture, sultanas, almonds, sugar and cinnamon.
5 Fold over about 2.5cm (1in) of the paste over the mixture on both of the shorter sides and brush with water.
6 Roll up the strudel, starting from one of the longer sides and use the teatowel to assist the rolling. Dampen the other long side and seal. Curve the strudel to form the shape of the letter C.
7 Carefully place the strudel on kitchen paper and slide onto a microwave baking tray or, if preferred, directly on the cooker shelf.
8 Cook for 6–7 min, turning halfway through the cooking time.
9 Leave to cool on a cooling rack. Sprinkle heavily with icing sugar. Serve in slices, hot or cold.

Alternative conventional bake
Cook on a baking tray in a preheated oven at 180°C (350°F) Mark 4 for 50–60 min.

100g (4oz) Strudel Paste (page 145)
15g (½oz) butter
25g (1oz) fresh breadcrumbs
1 lemon, grated rind
450g (1lb) cooking apples, peeled and shredded
1 × 15ml tbsp (1tbsp) oil
2 × 15ml tbsp (2tbsp) red jam, sieved
40g (1½oz) sultanas
50g (2oz) ground almonds
2 × 15ml tbsp (2tbsp) soft brown sugar
1 × 5ml tsp (1tsp) cinnamon
icing sugar for dredging

Crumbles and pies

Blackberry and apple crumble *(serves 4–6)*
POWER SETTING 7 (FULL OR HIGH)

1 Lightly grease a 1¼l (2pt) pie dish or large soufflé dish.
2 Peel, core and slice the apples, wash and dry the blackberries. Place the fruit in the bottom of the prepared dish with the caster sugar.
3 Sift the flour and salt, rub in the butter or margarine finely. Reserving 1 × 15ml tbsp (1tbsp) demerara sugar, stir the rest into the crumb mixture.
4 Sprinkle the crumb mixture lightly over the fruit and cook for 10–12 min, giving the dish a quarter turn every 3 min.
5 Sprinkle with the remaining demerara sugar and serve hot or cold with custard sauce or cream.

Alternative conventional bake
Cook in a preheated oven at 220°C (425°F) Mark 7 for about 45 min.

Variation
Use any fruit for the base but for a 'nuttier' texture, stir in 2 × 15ml tbsp (2tbsp) chopped walnuts into the crumb mixture before sprinkling over the fruit.

450g (1lb) cooking apples
225g (½lb) blackberries, fresh or frozen, thawed
100g (4oz) caster sugar
175g (6oz) plain flour
pinch salt
75g (3oz) butter or margarine
50g (2oz) demerara sugar
For serving:
Custard Sauce (page 146) or cream

Apple Strudel

105

675g (1½lb) dessert pears
sugar to taste
75g (3oz) plain flour
75g (3oz) wholemeal flour
pinch salt
75g (3oz) butter or margarine
50g (2oz) demerara sugar
50g (2oz) polka dots or
chocolate chips
For serving:
Rich Chocolate Sauce (page
146)

Pear and chocolate crumble (*serves 4–6*)
POWER SETTING 7 (FULL OR HIGH)

1 Lightly grease a 20–22.5cm (8–9in) round dish.
2 Peel, quarter and core the pears, and place into the base of the prepared dish. Sprinkle with sugar to taste.
3 Sift the plain flour, stir in the wholemeal flour and salt. Rub in the butter or margarine finely, stir in the demerara sugar and the polka dots or chocolate chips.
4 Sprinkle the mixture over the pears and cook for 10–12 min, giving a quarter turn every 3 min.
5 Serve with chocolate sauce.

Alternative conventional bake
Cook in a preheated oven at 190°C (375°F) Mark 5 for 50–55 min.

675g (1½lb) gooseberries
75–100g (3–4oz) sugar
25g (1oz) butter
½ × 5ml tsp (½tsp) cinnamon
100g (4oz) plain flour
pinch salt
50g (2oz) rolled oats
75g (3oz) butter or margarine
100g (4oz) demerara sugar
For serving:
Custard Sauce (page 146)

Crisp gooseberry pie (*serves 4–6*)
POWER SETTING 7 (FULL OR HIGH)

1 Top and tail and wash the gooseberries. Cover and cook them with the sugar, butter and cinnamon for 5–6 min until just soft. Drain off some of the juice and reserve. Place the fruit in 20–22.5cm (8–9in) dish and leave to cool.
2 Sift the flour with the salt, stir in the rolled oats and rub in the butter or margarine. Stir in the demerara sugar. This will make a coarse crumb mixture.
3 Sprinkle the mixture over the gooseberries and cook for 8–10 min until hot through and the topping is cooked. Turn two or three times throughout.
4 Serve hot or cold with custard sauce and serve the rest of the juice separately.

Alternative conventional bake
Cook in a preheated oven at 200°C (400°F) Mark 6 for 40–45 min.

675g (1½lb) blackcurrants,
fresh or frozen, thawed
75–100g (3–4oz) sugar
100g (4oz) self-raising flour
100g (4oz) wholemeal flour
pinch salt
½ × 5ml tsp (½tsp) baking
powder
50g (2oz) butter or margarine
25g (1oz) caster sugar
milk for mixing
demerara or soft brown sugar
for sprinkling
For serving:
cream

Blackcurrant cobbler (*serves 4–6*)
POWER SETTING 7 (FULL OR HIGH)

Cobbler is a scone mix topping – delicious with blackcurrants but almost any stewed fruit can be used

1 Pick over and wash the fresh blackcurrants if used. Cover and cook the blackcurrants with the sugar for 4–5 min until just soft. Drain off some of the juice and reserve. Place the fruit in a 17.5–20cm (7–8in) dish.
2 Sift the self-raising flour, add the wholemeal flour, and stir in the salt and baking powder. Rub in the butter or margarine finely, stir in the caster sugar. Mix to a soft scone dough with the milk.
3 Knead lightly on a floured surface and roll out to 1.25cm (½in) thick. Cut into rounds with a 5cm (2in) cutter.
4 Arrange the scone rounds over the top of the fruit and brush with milk. Sprinkle with the sugar.
5 Cook for 5–6 min, turning twice throughout.
6 Serve hot or cold with cream and serve the reserved fruit juice separately.

Alternative conventional bake
Cook in a preheated oven at 200°C (400°F) Mark 6 for 20–25 min.

Pear and Chocolate Crumble with Rice Chocolate Sauce

450g (1lb) cooking apples

3 × 15ml tbsp (3tbsp) demerara sugar

25g (1oz) butter, melted

50g (2oz) sultanas

6 slices white bread

100g (4oz) butter

2 × 15ml tbsp (2tbsp) demerara sugar

For serving:

cream or Custard Sauce (page 146)

Apple and sultana charlotte *(serves 4–6)*

POWER SETTING 7 (FULL OR HIGH)

1 Lightly grease a 20–22.5cm (8–9in) round dish.
2 Peel, core and slice the apples and layer into the base of the prepared dish with the sugar, melted butter and sultanas. Cover and cook for 4–5 min turning once halfway through.
3 Cut the bread slices into quarters. Melt the butter for 2–3 min and dip in the bread.
4 Preheat a browning dish for 5–6 min and cook half the bread for 1 min each side until lightly browned. Preheat the browning dish for a further 2–3 min and cook the remaining bread.
5 Arrange the toasted bread over the apples and sprinkle with brown sugar.
6 Heat through for about 2 min and serve hot with the cream or custard sauce.

Alternative conventional bake
The bread slices may be dipped in butter and then fried in a frying pan before arranging over the apples and heating through in the microwave cooker. Alternatively, arrange the bread slices dipped in butter over the apples and cook in a preheated oven at 190°C (375°F) Mark 5 for 35–40 min until crisp and brown.

Variation
When plentiful, pears make a good alternative to the apples.

Peaches and cream pie (serves 8–10)
POWER SETTING 4 (DEFROST OR MEDIUM)

1 Halve and slice the peaches and arrange in the bottom of a 22.5cm (9in) dish. Sprinkle with caster sugar (use less if the peaches are canned) and the cinnamon.
2 Beat the eggs with the cream and pour over the peaches. Cook for 12–15 min on setting 4 (defrost or medium) until set, giving a quarter turn every 3 min.
3 Mix together the flours and salt. Rub in the butter and stir in the demerara sugar to give a coarse crumb mixture.
4 Sprinkle the crumb mixture over the peaches and cream and cook on setting 4 (defrost or medium) for 7–8 min until the crumb topping is cooked.
5 Leave to cool slightly and serve with whipped cream, or when cold, pipe with whipped cream.

Alternative conventional bake
Add the eggs and cream to the peaches, scatter with the topping and cook in a preheated oven at 180°C (350°F) Mark 4 for 50–60 min.

Note: *Do not freeze this dish.*

900g (2lb) peaches, fresh or canned, drained
50–100g (2–4oz) caster sugar
$\frac{1}{2} \times$ 5ml tsp ($\frac{1}{2}$tsp) cinnamon
2 eggs, beaten
150ml ($\frac{1}{4}$pt) soured cream
25g (1oz) plain flour
50g (2oz) wholemeal flour
pinch salt
75g (3oz) butter
75g (3oz) demerara sugar
For decoration:
whipped cream

Black cherry and cream cheese pancake pie (serves 6)
POWER SETTING 7 (FULL OR HIGH)

1 Cream the cheese, add the caster sugar and beat well together until light and fluffy. Fold in the whipped cream.
2 Warm the jam for 2–3 min, stir with a wooden spoon. If the pancakes are freshly made, keep them warm; otherwise cover them and heat through for 3–4 min. Melt the butter for 1 min.
3 Spread the hot pancakes with the jam and cream cheese mixture, layer them in a serving dish ending with a pancake on top. Pour over the melted butter.
4 Cover and heat through for $\frac{1}{2}$–1 min. Serve straight away cut into wedges with whipped cream.

Alternative conventional bake
Heat through in a preheated oven at 180°C (350°F) Mark 4 for about 10 min.

225g ($\frac{1}{2}$lb) cream cheese
25g (1oz) caster sugar
75ml ($\frac{1}{8}$pt) double cream, whipped
225g ($\frac{1}{2}$lb) black cherry jam
8–10 Pancakes (page 114)
25g (1oz) butter
For serving:
whipped cream

Brown betty (serves 4–6)
POWER SETTING 7 (FULL OR HIGH)

1 Lightly grease a 15–17.5cm (6–7in) round dish.
2 Place the rhubarb, demerara sugar and orange juice into a bowl covered with clingfilm or alternatively a boiling or roasting bag loosely sealed.
3 Cook for 5–6 min, stirring or shaking twice throughout. Leave to cool slightly.
4 Melt the butter for 2–3 min and toss in the breadcrumbs ensuring they are evenly coated with the butter.
5 Preheat the browning dish for 7–8 min, add the breadcrumbs and cook for 2–3 min until lightly browned, stirring frequently. Mix in the grated orange rind.
6 Place a third of the rhubarb in the prepared dish, cover with a third of the

450g (1lb) rhubarb, washed and cut into 2.5cm (1in) pieces
100g (4oz) demerara sugar
1 orange, juice and grated rind
100g (4oz) butter
100g (4oz) white breadcrumbs
demerara sugar for sprinkling
For serving:
cream or Custard Sauce (page 146)

crumbs. Continue the layers, finishing with a layer of crumbs. Sprinkle with demerara sugar.

7 Heat through in the microwave for 3–4 min and serve hot with cream or custard sauce.

Alternative conventional bake
Fry the buttered crumbs in a frying pan until browned before layering with the fruit to heat through in the microwave cooker. Alternatively, layer the uncooked fruit, sugar and orange juice with the white breadcrumbs and orange rind, adding a little melted butter to each layer. Then cook in a preheated oven at 190°C (375°F) Mark 5 for 40–45 min.

Variation
Almost any fruit can be used but apples, gooseberries or plums are particularly good.

Brown Betty in preparation

Savoury dishes

Savoury flans, pies and puddings with plenty of filling are useful standbys in the freezer as there is a variety of ways in which they may be used. In portions they can be served as a first course to a meal or with vegetables or salad as the main course. Hot or cold, they make ideal snacks and are easily packed away for the picnic basket. Savoury pastries can be used for all sorts of occasions when entertaining and a variety of them may be served as main dishes for a buffet party.

Savoury quiches, stuffed pancakes and pizzas are good ways of using up leftovers in the refrigerator. They make substantial, nourishing and economical dishes and, when cooked in the microwave, they are even more economical! The techniques required for pastry making are given in the 'Pastry' section.

Traditionally pizzas were devised as a way of using up leftover bread dough and savoury morsels. If you are cooking a selection of pizzas and therefore are making up a batch of dough, I would suggest that you read the introductory pages of the section on 'Breads' as a useful guide.

Here then, are recipes for traditional and regional dishes together with some of my own favourites, and I hope that you will be encouraged to try them for yourselves.

Pizzas and pancakes

1 × 5ml tsp (1tsp) sugar
275ml (½pt) water, approximately
2 × 5ml tsp (2tsp) dried yeast
450g (1lb) plain flour
1½ × 5ml tsp (1½tsp) salt
3 × 15ml tbsp (3tbsp) olive oil

Pizza dough (*makes 3 large or 4 smaller pizzas*)
POWER SETTING 7 (FULL OR HIGH)

1 Lightly grease 3–4 × 20–25cm (8–10in) plates.
2 Add the sugar to half the water and heat for 30 sec. Stir in the yeast and leave to activate.
3 Sift the flour and salt and warm for 30 sec, warm the rest of the water for 30 sec.
4 Add the yeast mixture to the flour and mix to a soft dough with the rest of the water, adjusting the quantity if necessary. When the mixture is smooth, turn onto a floured surface and knead well.
5 Place the dough in a bowl, cover with clingfilm and prove by heating for 15 sec, then letting it rest for 5–10 min. Repeat 3–4 times until dough is double in size.
6 Knead the dough again, this time working in the oil, a little at a time until all the oil is absorbed and the dough is pliable and smooth.
7 Shape the dough by rolling or pressing into 3 larger or 4 smaller rounds to fit the prepared plates. Prove each round separately in rotation in the microwave as described above until well risen.

Quick pizza (*makes 3–4*)
POWER SETTING 7 (FULL OR HIGH)

This scone dough makes a good substitute for the bread dough when in a hurry; choose one of the toppings listed for traditional pizzas

1 Lightly grease 3–4 × 17.5–22.5cm (7–9in) plates.
2 Sift the flour, seasonings and baking powder into a bowl and rub in the butter or margarine finely.
3 Stir in the grated cheese and add sufficient milk to form a soft scone dough. Knead lightly on a floured surface.
4 Divide the mixture into 3 large or 4 smaller pieces and pat or roll into rounds. Place on the prepared plates.
5 Coat with the prepared chosen topping and cook each pizza for 4½–5½ min, giving a quarter turn every minute.

Alternative conventional bake
Place the dough rounds on greased baking trays or sandwich tins. Coat with the prepared chosen topping and cook in a preheated oven at 200°C (400°F) Mark 6 for 15 min, then reduce to 190°C (375°F) Mark 5 for a further 15–20 min.

350g (¾lb) self-raising flour
½ × 5ml tsp (½tsp) salt
pinch pepper
pinch dry mustard
1 × 5ml tsp (1tsp) baking powder
75g (3oz) butter or margarine
75–100g (3–4oz) cheese, finely grated
150ml (¼pt) milk or milk and water to mix
pizza topping (page 114)

Pizza napolitana
POWER SETTING 7 (FULL OR HIGH)

1 Follow the method for the pizza dough. When the dough has been shaped and proved for the second time, add the topping.
2 Spread each round of dough liberally with the tomato sauce. Cover with the cheese which has been thinly sliced, the drained anchovy fillets which have been split in two lengthways, and the black olives.
3 Sprinkle with the herbs and the olive oil (about 1–2 × 5ml tsp/1–2tsp) for each pizza.
4 Cook the smaller pizzas for 5–6 min each, the larger ones for 7–8 min each, giving a quarter turn every 1½ min.

Alternative conventional bake
If using metal bakeware to cook the pizzas conventionally, do not prove the second time in the microwave cooker, but leave to rise in a warm place for 20–30 min. Place in a preheated oven at 200°C (400°F) Mark 6 for 15 min then reduce heat to 190°C (375°F) Mark 5 for a further 15–20 min.

450g (1lb) Pizza Dough (page 112)
550ml (1pt) Tomato Sauce (page 148)
350g (¾lb) mozzarella cheese
50g (2oz) can anchovy fillets
75–100g (3–4oz) black olives
1–2 × 5ml tsp (1–2tsp) dried herbs eg oregano, basil or marjoram
2 × 15ml tbsp (2tbsp) olive oil, approximately

Variations

Pizza alla romana Omit the tomato sauce and anchovies and replace with extra mozzarella cheese and sprinkle liberally with grated parmesan cheese and fresh basil.

Pizza aglioe olio Omit the tomato sauce and cheese and replace with liberal amounts of crushed or finely chopped garlic, olive oil and chopped marjoram.

Onion pizza Follow the ingredients for Pizza Napolitana but add some lightly sautéed onion rings to the top with the anchovies and olives.

Mushroom pizza Omit the anchovies and olives and replace with lightly sautéed sliced mushrooms.

Seafood pizza Omit the cheese and replace with shelled mussels or prawns; sprinkle with oregano and chopped parsley.

American pizza Follow the ingredients for Pizza Napolitana, adding slices of salami on top of the cheese and slices of red pepper, lightly sautéed in oil.

Ham pizza Follow the ingredients for Pizza Napolitana adding some sliced ham and mortadella sausage which have been thinly shredded.

100g (4oz) plain flour
pinch salt
1 egg, beaten
275ml (½pt) milk
oil for frying

Pancakes

Pancakes cannot be successfully cooked in the microwave so are best cooked conventionally; this basic pancake batter is sufficient to make 8–10 thin pancakes

1 Sift the flour and salt into a mixing bowl. Make a well in the centre and drop in the beaten egg.
2 Slowly pour on half the milk, mixing the egg and milk into the flour with a wooden spoon.
3 Beat the mixture with a wooden spoon or whisk until smooth and free of lumps.
4 Add the remaining milk, whisking continually until the mixture is bubbly and the consistency of single cream.
5 Heat a 17.5–20cm (7–8in) frying pan on a conventional hotplate or burner. Just sufficient oil should be added to prevent the pancakes from sticking.
6 The pan and oil should be really hot. Pour in just enough batter to allow a thin film to coat the base of the pan, tilting the pan to spread the mixture.
7 The base of the pancake should be cooked in about 1 min. Flip the pancake over with a palette knife or spatula and cook the other side for about 1 min. If the pancakes are taking too long to cook, adjust the heat or make sure that too much batter is not being used.
8 Layer the pancakes in absorbent kitchen paper and keep warm if to be used immediately. Alternatively leave to cool, or freeze as they may be thawed and reheated most satisfactorily in the microwave.
9 Fill and use as required, allowing one per person if served as a starter to a meal or two if served as a snack or as a main course with vegetables.

(left) *Seafood Pizza and* (right) *Ham Pizza*

50g (2oz) button mushrooms

1 × 5ml tsp (1tsp) butter

225g (½lb) cooked chicken, chopped

275ml (½pt) Béchamel Sauce (page 147)

salt and freshly ground black pepper

1 × 15ml tbsp (1tbsp) chopped parsley

8 Pancakes (page 114)

25g (1oz) butter

parmesan cheese for sprinkling

Chicken pancakes
POWER SETTING 7 (FULL OR HIGH)

These are delicious served as a snack or supper dish but can also be served as a first course to a meal; the filling is sufficient to fill 8 pancakes – depending on how they are to be served allow one or two per person

1 Wash and slice the mushrooms, place in a dish with the 1 × 5ml tsp (1tsp) butter, cover and cook for 1½–2 min. Drain off any excess liquid.
2 Add the mushrooms and the chicken to the sauce, season well and stir in the parsley.
3 If the sauce is cold, heat in the microwave for 2–3 min or until hot.
4 Divide the mixture between the pancakes then fold in or roll up each one. Arrange on the serving plate or dish.
5 Melt the butter for 1 min and pour over the pancakes. Sprinkle with the parmesan cheese.
6 Cover the pancakes with clingfilm, making a slit with the pointed end of a sharp knife and heat through for 2½–3½ min.
7 Remove clingfilm and serve hot.

Alternative conventional bake
Heat through under a slow grill or covered in a preheated oven at 180°C (350°F) Mark 4 for 15–20 min.

Variation
Cooked meat, eg ham or chopped crispy bacon, or diced hardboiled egg can replace the cooked chicken.

Note: *Do not freeze pancakes with hardboiled egg in the filling.*

2–3 × 15ml tbsp (2–3tbsp) sweetcorn

225g (½lb) cooked fish, eg fresh or smoked cod or haddock, flaked

275ml (½pt) Béchamel Sauce (page 147)

salt and freshly ground black pepper

few drops of lemon juice

8 Pancakes (page 114)

3–4 × 15ml tbsp (3–4tbsp) grated cheese, eg emmenthal or gruyère

For serving:

lemon wedges and sprig of parsley

Fish pancakes
POWER SETTING 7 (FULL OR HIGH)

1 Add the sweetcorn and the fish to the sauce, add seasonings to taste and lemon juice.
2 If the sauce is cold, heat in the microwave for 2–3 min or until hot.
3 Divide the mixture between the pancakes, then fold in or roll up each one. Arrange on the serving dish or plate. Sprinkle with grated cheese.
4 Cover and heat through as for chicken pancakes.
5 Serve hot with lemon wedges and a sprig of parsley.

Alternative conventional bake
As for Chicken Pancakes.

Variation
Salmon, tuna fish or prawns can replace the cod or haddock.

Spinach pancakes
POWER SETTING 7 (FULL OR HIGH)

1 Add the spinach to the sauce with seasonings to taste. Stir in the grated cheese and heat for 2–3 min or until hot.
2 Divide the mixture between the pancakes, then fold in or roll up each one. Arrange on the serving dish or plate. Cover and heat through as for chicken pancakes.
3 Warm the soured cream for 15–30 sec. Pour over the pancakes and sprinkle with parsley.
4 Serve immediately.

Alternative conventional bake
As for Chicken Pancakes.

Variation
Almost any cooked vegetable can be used for this dish as an alternative to the spinach – asparagus tips are especially good.

Savoury pancake pie

Follow the ingredients and method for any one or more of the fillings and layer the pancakes in rounds with the fillings in between in a deep dish. Heat through with a cheese sauce poured over or heat through covered, then pour over some soured cream. Sprinkle with chopped parsley or paprika pepper and to serve cut into wedges like a cake.

225g (½lb) cooked fresh or frozen spinach, chopped
275ml (½pt) Béchamel Sauce (page 147)
salt and freshly ground black pepper
4 × 15ml tbsp (4tbsp) grated cheese
8 Pancakes (page 114)
For serving:
soured cream and chopped parsley

Flans, tarts and quiches

Mushroom flan *(serves 6)*
POWER SETTING 7 (FULL OR HIGH) OR 4 (DEFROST OR MEDIUM)

1 Roll out the pastry, line a 20cm (8in) flan dish and bake blind (page 142).
2 Melt the butter or margarine in a large bowl for 1 min, add the onion and the mushrooms, toss well, cover and cook for 4–5 min.
3 Drain off the liquid and reserve some slices of mushroom for garnish.
4 Beat the double cream and eggs into the béchamel sauce. Add the seasonings, onion and mushrooms.
5 Pour the mixture into the flan case and cook for 7–8 min giving a quarter turn every 2 min. If not quite set, 15–30 sec heating periods can be given until set, but usually the filling will set during a 15–20 min standing period after removal from the oven. Alternatively cook on setting 4 (defrost or medium) for 14–16 min turning every 3 min.
6 Serve hot or cold garnished with the reserved mushroom slices and chopped parsley.

Alternative conventional bake
It is not necessary to bake the pastry case first. Cook the complete dish in a preheated oven at 190°C (375°F) Mark 5 for 40–50 min.

175g (6oz) Light Wholemeal Pastry (page 144)
25g (1oz) butter or margarine
1 medium onion, peeled and finely sliced
350g (¾lb) mushrooms, washed and finely sliced
2 × 15ml tbsp (2tbsp) double cream
2 eggs, beaten
275ml (½pt) Béchamel Sauce (page 147)
salt and pepper to taste
chopped parsley for garnish

Mum
Don't forget
Pancake day
love
Kate xx

Sweetcorn and onion flan (serves 6)
POWER SETTING 7 (FULL OR HIGH) OR 4 (DEFROST OR MEDIUM)

175g (6oz) Light Wholemeal Pastry (page 144)
25g (1oz) butter or margarine
1 large onion, peeled and finely sliced
75ml ($\frac{1}{8}$pt) milk, approximately
325g (11$\frac{1}{2}$oz) can sweetcorn
2 eggs, beaten
salt and pepper to taste
75g (3oz) cheese, finely grated

1 Roll out the pastry, line a 20cm (8in) flan dish and bake blind (page 142).
2 Melt the butter or margarine for 1 min in a bowl, add the onion, toss well and cook for 4–5 min until soft. Drain the liquid and make up to 150ml ($\frac{1}{4}$pt) with the milk, add to the onions.
3 Add the contents of the can of sweetcorn, eggs, seasoning and half the cheese to the onions and the milk. Mix well together.
4 Pour into the flan case and sprinkle with the remaining cheese.
5 Cook for 7–8 min, giving a quarter turn every 2 min. If not quite set, 15–30 sec heating periods can be given until set, but usually the filling will set during a 15–20 min standing period after removal from the oven. Alternatively, cook on setting 4 (defrost or medium) for 14–16 min turning every 3 min.
6 Serve hot or cold with salad.

Alternative conventional bake
It is not necessary to bake the pastry case first. Cook the complete dish in a preheated oven at 190°C (375°F) Mark 5 for 40–50 min.

Variations
For Sweetcorn and Tuna Flan, use a small onion and can of sweetcorn but add 200g (7oz) can of tuna fish, drained and flaked.

Asparagus flan (serves 6)
POWER SETTING 7 (FULL OR HIGH) AND 4 (DEFROST OR MEDIUM)

175g (6oz) Light Wholemeal Pastry (page 144)
25g (1oz) butter or margarine
1 small onion, peeled and finely chopped
290g (10$\frac{1}{2}$oz) can condensed asparagus soup
3 eggs, beaten
3 × 15ml tbsp (3tbsp) single cream or top of the milk
salt and pepper to taste
100g (4oz) cheese, grated
For decoration:
10–12 canned, frozen or fresh cooked asparagus spears

1 Roll out the pastry, line a 20cm (8in) flan dish and bake blind (page 142).
2 Melt the butter or margarine in a bowl for 1 min, toss in the chopped onion and cook for 2–3 min until soft.
3 Beat together the soup, eggs, cream and seasonings until smooth and well blended. Stir in the cooked onion.
4 Cook the mixture on setting 4 (defrost or medium) for 6–8 min until heated through, whisking every 2 min. Stir in the cheese.
5 Pour into the cooked flan case and cook on setting 4 (defrost or medium) for 11–13 min, turning every 3 min. Allow to stand for a few minutes.
6 Heat the asparagus spears for 1–1$\frac{1}{2}$ min and arrange on the top of the flan.
7 Serve on its own as a snack or with potatoes and salad as a main meal.

Alternative conventional bake
When the filling is added to the cooked flan case, cook in a preheated oven at 180°C (350°F) Mark 4 for 20–25 min until set and lightly browned.

Asparagus Pancakes

119

175g (6oz) Light Wholemeal Pastry (page 144)

25g (1oz) butter or margarine

1 medium onion, peeled and finely sliced

1–2 × 5ml tsp (1–2tsp) curry powder

275ml (½pt) Béchamel Sauce (page 147)

150ml (¼pt) soured cream

salt and pepper to taste

225g (½lb) peeled prawns

50g (2oz) long-grained rice, cooked

paprika pepper for sprinkling

Indian-style flan *(serves 6)*
POWER SETTING 7 (FULL OR HIGH)

1 Roll out the pastry, line a 20cm (8in) flan dish and bake blind (page 142).
2 Melt the butter or margarine in a bowl, add the onion, toss well and cook for 2–3 min until soft and transparent. Stir in the curry powder and cook for a further minute.
3 Stir in the béchamel sauce, soured cream and seasoning. Reserving a few prawns for garnish, stir the remainder into the sauce.
4 Pour the mixture into the flan case and smooth the top.
5 Arrange the reserved prawns on the top and the cooked rice around the edge of the flan. Sprinkle with paprika pepper.
6 Serve cold with a crisp salad.

Note: *If freezing this dish, do not garnish with the rice. Finish and decorate just before serving.*

175g (6oz) Rich Shortcrust Pastry (page 144)

225g (½lb) white fish eg cod or haddock fillets

few drops lemon juice

25g (1oz) butter or margarine

1 medium onion, peeled and finely sliced

25g (1oz) flour

150ml (¼pt) milk

salt and pepper to taste

3 eggs, beaten

4 tomatoes, skinned

25–50g (1–2oz) cheese, finely grated

paprika pepper for sprinkling

White fish flan *(serves 6)*
POWER SETTING 7 (FULL OR HIGH) OR 4 (DEFROST OR MEDIUM)

1 Roll out the pastry, line a 20cm (8in) flan dish and bake blind (page 142).
2 Put the fish into a dish or on a plate, sprinkle with lemon juice, cover and cook for 2–2½ min, turning once halfway through.
3 Drain the fish, reserving juices. Flake the fish discarding any bones or skin.
4 Melt the butter or margarine for 1 min in a bowl, add the onion, toss well and cook for 2–3 min until soft and transparent. Stir in the flour and gradually add the milk and reserved juices. Mix well and season to taste.
5 Cook for 2–3 min, stirring every minute until thickened. Leave to cool slightly before beating in the eggs.
6 Slice the tomatoes thinly and arrange with the fish in the bottom of the flan case. Season well.
7 Pour over the sauce, smooth the top and sprinkle with the grated cheese and paprika.
8 Cook for 4 min, giving a quarter turn every minute. Allow to stand for 5 min, then cook for a further 2 min. Alternatively, cook on setting 4 (defrost or medium) for 14–16 min, turning every 3 min. If not quite set, heat for 15–30 sec periods or allow to stand after removal from the oven for 15–20 min.
9 Serve on its own as a snack or with potatoes and a green vegetable as a main meal.

Alternative conventional bake
When filling is added to the flan case, cook in a preheated oven at 190°C (375°F) Mark 5 for 20–25 min until set and golden brown.

Cheese and onion flan *(serves 6)*
POWER SETTING 7 (FULL OR HIGH)

1 Roll out the pastry, line a 20cm (8in) flan dish and bake blind (page 142). Reserve the trimmings.
2 Melt the butter in a large bowl for 1 min. Add the onions and toss well in the butter.
3 Cover and cook for 8–9 min until soft, shaking or stirring twice throughout.
4 Add the cheese to the onions with the salt and black pepper. Mix well together and place into the flan case.
5 Roll out the trimmings from the pastry and cut into thin strips. Lay the strips of pastry over the filling in a lattice style.
6 Cook for 3 min, rest for 3 min. Turn the dish and cook for a further 2–3 min or until lattice is cooked and set.
7 Leave to stand for a few minutes and then sprinkle with paprika pepper.
8 Serve hot or cold as a snack or part of a main course.

Alternative conventional bake
It is not necessary to cook the pastry case first. Cook the complete dish in a preheated oven at 190°C (375°F) Mark 5 for 35–40 min.

225g (½lb) Light Wholemeal Pastry (page 144)
25g (1oz) butter or margarine
450g (1lb) onions, peeled and finely sliced
175g (6oz) strong cheddar cheese, grated
salt and freshly ground black pepper
paprika pepper for sprinkling

Smoked fish flan *(serves 6)*
POWER SETTING 7 (FULL OR HIGH) AND 4 (DEFROST OR MEDIUM)

1 Roll out the pastry, line a 20cm (8in) flan dish and bake blind (page 142).
2 Place the leek in a boiling or roasting bag or covered casserole dish with a sprinkling of salt and 2–3 × 15ml tbsp (2–3tbsp) water and cook for 4–5 min. Drain off the water.
3 Flake the fish discarding any bones or skin and place in the bottom of the flan case with the leek.
4 Arrange the slices of hardboiled egg on the top, sprinkle with salt and pepper and cover with the béchamel sauce.
5 Beat half the cheese into the potato and place the mixture in a forcing bag with a large star nozzle. Pipe the potato around the edge and across the middle of the flan.
6 Heat through on setting 4 (defrost or medium) for 9–10 min, turning every 3–4 min.
7 Sprinkle with the remaining cheese and cook for 1 min until the cheese is melted. Alternatively brown under a hot grill.
8 Serve garnished with parsley.

Alternative conventional bake
When the filling is added to the flan case, cook in a preheated oven at 190°C (375°F) Mark 5 for 25–30 min until heated through and the potato is lightly browned.

Note: *This dish is not suitable for freezing.*

175g (6oz) Rich Shortcrust Pastry (page 144)
1 medium leek, washed and finely sliced
salt and pepper to taste
225g (½lb) smoked cod or haddock, cooked
2 hardboiled eggs, sliced
275ml (½pt) Béchamel Sauce (page 147)
50g (2oz) cheese, finely grated
450g (1lb) creamed potatoes
parsley for garnishing

175g (6oz) Rich Shortcrust
Pastry (page 144)

150ml ($\frac{1}{4}$pt) Béchamel Sauce
(page 147)

salt and pepper to taste

225g ($\frac{1}{2}$lb) crabmeat, fresh or
frozen

150ml ($\frac{1}{4}$pt) mayonnaise

few drops lemon juice

2 hardboiled eggs, chopped

150ml ($\frac{1}{4}$pt) double cream,
whipped

For decoration:

thinly sliced cucumber and
chopped parsley

Seafood flan *(serves 6)*
POWER SETTING 7 (FULL OR HIGH)

1 Roll out the pastry, line a 20cm (8in) flan dish and bake blind (page 142).
Leave to cool.
2 Beat the béchamel sauce and add seasoning. Mix in the crabmeat, mayonnaise, lemon juice and chopped hardboiled egg. Finally fold in the whipped double cream.
3 Pour the mixture into the cooled flan case and smooth the top. Chill until set.
4 Serve cold garnished with cucumber slices and chopped parsley as a starter to a meal or as a main course with mixed salad.

Note: *This dish is not suitable for freezing.*

Variations
Cooked and shelled prawns, scampi, mussels, scallops, lobster, fresh or canned tuna or salmon or a mixture of these can be used as alternatives to the crabmeat.

Seafood Flan

122

175g (6oz) Light Wholemeal
Pastry (page 144)

1 medium onion, peeled

1–2 cloves garlic

275g (10oz) cooked ham

2 × 5ml tsp (2tsp) dried
herbs, eg oregano, basil

freshly ground black pepper

3 eggs, beaten

150ml (¼pt) milk

50g (2oz) cheese, grated

parmesan cheese for
sprinkling

paprika pepper for sprinkling,
optional

tomato slices for garnish

Ham tart (serves 6)
POWER SETTING 4 (DEFROST OR MEDIUM)

1 Roll out the pastry, line a 20cm (8in) flan dish and bake blind (page 142).
2 Mince the onion, garlic and ham. Mix well together and add the herbs, pepper, eggs, milk and grated cheese.
3 Cook the mixture on setting 4 (defrost or medium) for 7–8 min or until heated through, stirring every 2 min.
4 Pour into the flan case and cook on setting 4 (defrost or medium) for 11–13 min, turning every 3 min. Allow to stand for a few minutes.
5 Sprinkle with parmesan cheese and paprika pepper; alternatively, sprinkle with parmesan cheese and brown the top under a hot grill.
6 Serve hot or cold garnished with tomato slices.

Alternative conventional bake
When the filling is added to the flan case, cook in a preheated oven at 180°C (350°F) Mark 4 for 20–25 min until set and lightly browned. Sprinkle with parmesan cheese and garnish with tomato slices.

Variation
Cooked chicken or turkey can be used instead of the ham.

175g (6oz) Rich Shortcrust
Pastry (page 144)

25g (1oz) butter or margarine

1 medium onion, peeled and
finely sliced

2 × 15ml tbsp (2tbsp) olive
oil

225g (½lb) aubergine, finely
sliced

1–2 cloves garlic, crushed or
finely chopped

2 eggs, beaten

150ml (¼pt) natural yoghurt or
milk

2 × 5ml tsp (2tsp) dried
herbs, eg oregano or basil

2 × 15ml tbsp (2tbsp) tomato
purée

salt and freshly ground black
pepper

Aubergine tart (serves 6)
POWER SETTING 7 (FULL OR HIGH) AND 4 (DEFROST OR MEDIUM)

1 Roll out the pastry, line a 20cm (8in) flan dish and bake blind (page 142).
2 Melt the butter or margarine for 1 min in a large bowl, add the onions, mix well together and cook for 2 min.
3 Add the oil, sliced aubergines and garlic, coat well in the butter and oil. Cover the dish and cook for a further 5–6 min until the onions and aubergines are soft, turning or shaking twice throughout. Keep warm.
4 Beat the eggs with the yoghurt or milk, add the herbs, tomato purée and seasoning. Add this to the onions and aubergines and heat on setting 4 (defrost or medium) for 3–4 min until hot, stirring every minute.
5 Pour into the flan case and cook on setting 4 (defrost or medium) for 10–12 min until set.
6 Serve hot or cold with crusty french bread.

Alternative conventional bake
When the filling is added to the flan case, cook in a preheated oven at 180°C (350°F) Mark 4 for 20–25 min until set.

Variation
For Courgette Tart, replace the aubergines with finely sliced courgettes or baby marrows.

Cream cheese tart *(serves 6)*
POWER SETTING 7 (FULL OR HIGH) AND 4 (DEFROST OR MEDIUM)

1 Roll out the pastry, line a 20cm (8in) flan dish and bake blind (page 142).
2 Beat the cream cheese, add the eggs gradually, beating well after each addition.
3 Stir in the natural yoghurt or milk, seasoning, parsley and ham.
4 Cook on setting 4 (defrost or medium) for 8 min, until hot, stirring every 2 min. Pour into the flan case.
5 Cook on setting 4 (defrost or medium) for 8–9 min, turning the dish twice throughout.
6 Slice the cheese very thinly – a vegetable peeler can be used – and arrange over the surface of the flan. Cook for a further 1–2 min until the cheese is just melted.
7 Sprinkle with chopped chives or parsley and serve hot or cold.

Alternative conventional bake
When the filling is added to the flan case, cook in a preheated oven at 180°C (350°F) Mark 4 for 20–25 min until set. Arrange the cheese over the surface and place back into the oven for a further 5 min.

Note: *This dish is not suitable for freezing.*

175g (6oz) Rich Shortcrust Pastry (page 144)
275g (10oz) cream cheese
3 eggs, beaten
150ml (¼pt) natural yoghurt or milk
salt and freshly ground black pepper
2 × 5ml tsp (2tsp) chopped parsley *or*
1 × 5ml tsp (1tsp) dried parsley
50g (2oz) ham, chopped
25g (1oz) cheese
chopped chives or parsley for sprinkling

Quiche Lorraine *(serves 6)*
POWER SETTING 7 (FULL OR HIGH) AND 4 (DEFROST OR MEDIUM)

1 Roll out the pastry, line a 20cm (8in) flan dish and bake blind (page 142).
2 Trim the bacon rashers and cut into 2.5cm (1in) strips. Place on kitchen paper and heat for 1–1½ min until just cooked.
3 Slice the cheese thinly (by using a vegetable peeler).
4 Arrange the bacon over the base of the flan case and place the cheese over the top.
5 Beat the eggs with the egg yolk, beat in the seasoning, milk and cream and pour into the flan case. Sprinkle with nutmeg or paprika.
6 Cook on setting 4 (defrost or medium) for 14–16 min, giving a quarter turn every 3 min. If not quite set, extra 15–30 sec heating periods can be given although the quiche will normally set during a 15–20 min standing period after removal from the oven.
7 Serve hot or cold with a crisp salad.

Alternative conventional bake
It is not necessary to bake the pastry case first. Cook the complete dish in a preheated oven at 190°C (375°F) Mark 5 for 30–40 min or until set.

175g (6oz) Rich Shortcrust Pastry (page 144)
4 rashers lean bacon
50g (2oz) cheese
2 eggs, beaten
1 egg yolk, beaten
salt and pepper to taste
150ml (¼pt) milk and top of the milk or single cream mixed
grated nutmeg or paprika for sprinkling

175g (6oz) Rich Shortcrust Pastry (page 144)

425ml (¾pt) Béchamel Sauce (page 147)

2 × 15ml tbsp (2tbsp) double cream

3 eggs, beaten

175g (6oz) gruyère cheese, grated

salt and pepper to taste

grated nutmeg for sprinkling

Swiss quiche (serves 6)
POWER SETTING 7 (FULL OR HIGH) OR 4 (DEFROST OR MEDIUM)

1 Roll out the pastry, line a 20cm (8in) flan dish and bake blind (page 142).
2 Whisk the béchamel sauce, gradually whisking in the cream and eggs. Stir in the grated cheese and add seasoning to taste.
3 Pour the mixture into the flan case and sprinkle with grated nutmeg.
4 Cook for 7–8 min turning every 2 min and allowing a 5 min rest period halfway through. Alternatively cook on setting 4 (defrost or medium) for 14–16 min. If not quite set, heat for 15–30 sec periods or allow to stand after removal from the oven for 15–20 min.
5 Serve with salad and crusty french bread or as a starter to a meal.

Alternative conventional bake
It is not necessary to bake the pastry flan case first. Cook the complete dish in a preheated oven at 190°C (375°F) Mark 5 for 40–50 min.

175g (6oz) Rich Shortcrust Pastry (page 144)

3 × 15ml tbsp (3tbsp) olive oil

2 large onions, peeled and finely sliced

1–2 cloves garlic, crushed or finely chopped

225g (½lb) can tomatoes

1 × 15ml tbsp (1tbsp) tomato purée

2 × 5ml tsp (2tsp) mixed chopped herbs, eg basil, oregano, thyme

salt and freshly ground black pepper

1 × 5ml tsp (1tsp) caster sugar

50g (2oz) can anchovy fillets

50–75g (2–3oz) black olives

Pissaladière (serves 6)
POWER SETTING 7 (FULL OR HIGH) AND 6 (ROAST OR MEDIUM/HIGH)

This strongly flavoured tart is characteristic of dishes from southern France and is similar to the Italian pizza but with a lighter pastry base. It makes a substantial lunch or supper dish served on its own or with crusty bread.

1 Roll out the pastry, line a 20cm (8in) flan dish and bake blind (page 142).
2 Place the oil, onions and garlic into a large bowl and toss well. Cover and cook for 5–6 min until the onions are soft and transparent. Shake or stir twice throughout. Drain off the liquid.
3 Roughly chop the tomatoes and place in a bowl with the tomato purée, herbs, seasoning and sugar. Stir and boil in the microwave until the liquid quantity is reduced and the mixture is fairly thick.
4 Add the tomato mixture to the drained onions and pour into the pastry case.
5 Drain the anchovy fillets and cut in half lengthwise. Arrange over the top of the flan in a lattice design. Garnish with the olives.
6 Cook on variable power control setting 6 (roast or medium/high) for 8–10 min until heated through thoroughly. Alternatively, heat through on full or high setting for 3 min, allow to stand for 3 min, repeat until hot through.
7 Serve hot with crusty french bread or garlic bread.

Alternative conventional bake
When the filling is added to the flan case, cook in a preheated oven at 200°C (400°F) Mark 6 for 20–25 min.

Pissaladière with Garlic Bread

Puddings and pies

225g (½lb) short cut macaroni

2 × 5ml tsp (2tsp) oil

1 × 5ml tsp (1tsp) salt

550ml (1pt) boiling water, approximately

350g (¾lb) cooked chicken, minced

100g (4oz) ham, minced

150ml (¼pt) top of the milk *or* milk and single cream

2 × 5ml tsp (2tsp) dried sage, thyme or basil

3 eggs, separated

1½ × 15ml tbsp (1½tbsp) tomato purée

salt and freshly ground black pepper

50g (2oz) cheddar cheese, grated

1 × 15ml tbsp (1tbsp) parmesan cheese

Chicken pasta pie (*serves 4–6*)
POWER SETTING 7 (FULL OR HIGH) AND 4 (DEFROST OR MEDIUM)

1 Well butter a 22.5cm (9in) round ovenware dish.
2 Place macaroni in a bowl with the oil and salt and pour on sufficient boiling water to cover. Stir, cover and cook for 8–10 min until plump and tender and most of the water has been absorbed. Stir twice.
3 Mix together the chicken, ham, milk, herbs, egg yolks, tomato purée and seasoning.
4 Whisk the egg whites until stiff and, with a metal spoon, fold into the meat mixture.
5 Rinse and drain the macaroni, place half in the bottom of the greased dish. Spread with the meat mixture and cover with the remaining macaroni.
6 Cover with clingfilm or a lid and cook on setting 4 (defrost or medium) for 15–18 min until cooked. Test the centre with a knife – the filling should be soft but set.
7 When cooked, leave to stand for 10–15 min. Sprinkle with the grated cheese and the parmesan cheese and serve hot.

Alternative conventional bake
Cover with foil and cook in a steamer over a pan of gently boiling water for 45–60 min. Alternatively, place the covered dish inside a larger dish containing hot water (water bath) and cook in a preheated oven at 180°C (350°F) Mark 4 for 45–60 min.

225g (½lb) aubergine, thinly sliced

salt

3 × 15ml tbsp (3tbsp) olive oil, approximately

1 large onion, peeled and finely sliced

450g (1lb) minced beef

1–2 cloves garlic, crushed or finely chopped

salt and freshly ground black pepper

1 × 15ml tbsp (1tbsp) tomato purée

400g (14oz) can tomatoes

1 × 5ml tsp (1tsp) dried oregano or basil

275ml (½pt) natural yoghurt

2 eggs, beaten

100g (4oz) cheese, grated

225g (½lb) short cut macaroni, cooked (see above)

Aubergine macaroni pie (*serves 4–6*)
POWER SETTING 7 (FULL OR HIGH) AND 4 (DEFROST OR MEDIUM)

1 Place the aubergine slices on a plate, sprinkle with salt and leave for 30 min. Rinse in cold water and dry.
2 Place in a large round casserole dish, sprinkle on the oil, cover and cook for 4–5 min until soft. Remove the slices onto a plate.
3 Add the onion to the casserole dish with a little more oil if necessary and cook for about 4 min until soft and transparent.
4 Add the minced beef, mix with the onion, cover and cook for 5–6 min until browned, stirring once or twice and breaking down any lumps with a fork.
5 Add the garlic, seasoning, tomato purée, tomatoes and herbs. Cover and cook for 10–15 min until tender, stirring twice throughout.
6 Wipe the sides of the dish and arrange the aubergine slices on the meat.
7 Mix together the yoghurt, beaten eggs, threequarters of the cheese and the cooked macaroni in a large bowl.
8 Cook on setting 4 (defrost or medium) for 4–5 min until hot. Pour the mixture over the aubergine slices.
9 Cook on setting 4 (defrost or medium) for 12–15 min until heated through and the topping is set.
10 Sprinkle with the remaining cheese and cook for 1–2 min until melted or alternatively, brown the top under a hot grill.

Alternative conventional bake
Cook in a preheated oven at 190°C (375°F) Mark 5 for 25–30 min until the top is browned.

Cottage pie (*serves 4–6*)
POWER SETTING 7 (FULL OR HIGH)

1 Melt the butter or margarine in a large round casserole for 1 min. Add the onion and cook for 2–3 min.
2 Add the minced beef, mix with the onion, cover and cook for 5–6 min until browned, stirring once or twice and breaking down any lumps with a fork.
3 Stir in the flour, stock, parsley, seasoning and worcestershire sauce. Cover and cook for 10–15 min, until tender, stirring every 5 min.
4 Wipe the sides of the dish and cover the meat with the potato, marking the surface with a fork. Alternatively, pipe the potato over the top using a large star nozzle fitted into a forcing bag.
5 Top with slivers of butter and cook until hot through (1–2 min if the ingredients are still hot, 5–6 min if cool). Sprinkle with paprika or brown top under a hot grill.

Alternative conventional bake
Place the potato over the meat and cook in a preheated oven at 190°C (375°F) Mark 5 for 30–35 min to heat through and brown the potato.

25g (1oz) butter or margarine
1 small onion, finely chopped
450g (1lb) minced beef
25g (1oz) flour
150ml (¼pt) beef stock
1 × 5ml tsp (1tsp) chopped parsley
salt and freshly ground black pepper
1 × 5ml tsp (1tsp) worcestershire sauce
450g (1lb) creamed potatoes
knob of butter
paprika pepper for sprinkling

Cheese pudding (*serves 4*)
POWER SETTING 7 (FULL OR HIGH)

This is a good light lunch or supper dish

1 Lightly grease a 15–17.5cm (6–7in) soufflé dish.
2 Remove the crusts from the bread, cut into dice and place in the greased dish.
3 Add the butter to the milk and warm for 2 min. Stir until the butter is melted.
4 Beat the eggs with the butter and milk, add the wine and season well. Pour over the bread.
5 Sprinkle over the cheese and paprika pepper.
6 Cook for 4–5 min, turning every 2 min.
7 Serve immediately.

Alternative conventional bake
Cook in a preheated oven at 190°C (375°F) Mark 5 for 30–35 min.

Note: *This dish is not suitable for freezing.*

6 medium slices brown bread
25g (1oz) butter
150ml (¼pt) milk
2 eggs, beaten
150ml (¼pt) dry white wine
salt and freshly ground black pepper
100g (4oz) cheese, grated
paprika pepper for sprinkling

Bacon and onion roly poly pudding (*serves 4–6*)
POWER SETTING 7 (FULL OR HIGH) AND 4 (DEFROST OR MEDIUM)

1 Trim the rind from the bacon rashers, place on a plate and cook for 2½–3 min. Drain off the fat, mix with the onion in a bowl and cook for 3–4 min, drain. Leave to cool.
2 Roll the pastry into a square 22.5 × 22.5cm (9 × 9in) and about 6mm (¼in) thick. Trim the edges if necessary.
3 Lay the bacon rashers over the pastry, sprinkle with the onions, herbs and pepper.
4 Roll up evenly sealing the top and edges.
5 Place the roly poly with the top edge down on a large piece of greased greaseproof paper. Roll the paper loosely around the pastry, allowing

225g (½lb) lean bacon rashers
1 medium onion, peeled and finely chopped
225g (½lb) Suet Crust Pastry (page 145)
1 × 5ml tsp (1tsp) chopped parsley
1 × 5ml tsp (1tsp) chopped sage
freshly ground black pepper

sufficient room for the pastry to rise. Secure the ends with string or rubber bands. Finally, cover with clingfilm.
6 Cook on setting 4 (defrost or medium) for 14–15 min until risen and cooked through. Test with a fine skewer pierced through the greaseproof paper. Alternatively, cook on full or high power for 4 min, rest for 5 min then cook for a further 3–4 min.
7 Remove clingfilm and greaseproof paper and serve hot with potatoes and either turnips, carrots or swede.

Alternative conventional bake
Wrap the roly poly loosely in greased aluminium foil or greaseproof paper, place in a steamer with lid over a pan of gently boiling water and steam for 1½–2 hrs.

Note: *This pudding is not really suitable for freezing.*

225g (½lb) flat noodles eg tagliatelle

2 × 5ml tsp (2tsp) oil

1 × 5ml tsp (1tsp) salt

550ml (1pt) boiling water, approximately

75g (3oz) butter or margarine, melted

350g (¾lb) cooked spinach, fresh or frozen

2 × 15ml tbsp (2tbsp) single cream *or* top of the milk

salt and freshly ground black pepper

25g (1oz) parmesan cheese, grated

For serving:

275ml (½pt) Cheese Sauce (page 148)

Layered noodle pudding *(serves 4–6)*
POWER SETTING 7 (FULL OR HIGH)

This dish may be served as a substantial snack or with a meat dish as part of a main course

1 Well butter a 850ml (1½pt) pudding basin.
2 Place the noodles in a bowl with the oil and salt and pour on sufficient boiling water to cover. Stir, cover and cook for 7–9 min until tender; stir twice.
3 Drain and rinse in hot running water. Drain well and stir in half the butter or margarine.
4 Mix well together the spinach, cream, seasonings, parmesan cheese and remaining butter or margarine.
5 Layer the buttered noodles and spinach mixture in the greased pudding basin, beginning and ending with a layer of noodles.
6 Cover with clingfilm, making a slit with the pointed end of a sharp knife. Cook for 5 min, turning every 2 min. Leave to stand for a few minutes.
7 Remove clingfilm, invert onto a hot serving plate or dish and serve with cheese sauce.

Alternative conventional bake
Cover with foil and steam over a pan of gently boiling water for 45–60 min or bake in a preheated oven at 180°C (350°F) Mark 4 for 20–25 min.

Asparagus Flan, Layered Noodle Pudding and Cheese Sauce

1 medium onion, peeled and
finely chopped
225g (½lb) streaky bacon
75g (3oz) red leicester cheese,
grated
1 × 5ml tsp (1tsp) dried
mixed herbs, optional
225g (½lb) Suet Crust Pastry
(page 145)

Leicester layered pudding (serves 5–6)
POWER SETTING 7 (FULL OR HIGH) AND 4 (DEFROST OR MEDIUM)

1 Line a 1¼l (2pt) pudding basin with clingfilm.
2 Place the onion in a bowl. Trim the rind and any bone from the bacon, cut into strips and add to the onion. Cover and cook for 3–4 min until softened. Drain off the liquid. Leave to cool.
3 Knead the herbs, if used, into the pastry. Cut the dough into halves; divide one half into 2; cut a small piece from the other half.
4 Roll out the smallest piece of dough and place in the bottom of the pudding basin, pressing down firmly. Sprinkle with some of the filling. Repeat the layers, graduating the sizes of pastry, finishing with the largest piece on top.
5 Cover with clingfilm, making a slit with the pointed end of a sharp knife.
6 Cook on setting 4 (defrost or medium) for 15–18 min, turning every 3–4 min.
7 Leave to stand for 10 min. Remove clingfilm, invert pudding onto a serving plate. Test pudding with a fine skewer, if not quite cooked, replace in the microwave for another 1–2 min.
8 Serve hot with a thick brown gravy and creamed potatoes.

Alternative conventional bake
Steam over a saucepan of gently boiling water for 1¾–2 hrs.

Note: *This pudding is not really suitable for freezing.*

450g (1lb) white fish fillets,
cooked
75g (3oz) white breadcrumbs
1 × 15ml tbsp (1tbsp)
chopped parsley
1 lemon, grated rind
salt and freshly ground black
pepper
50g (2oz) butter or margarine
2 eggs, beaten
For serving:
Tomato Sauce (page 148)

Fish pudding (serves 4–5)
POWER SETTING 7 (FULL OR HIGH)

This pudding is very light in texture and makes a good lunch or supper dish

1 Lightly grease a 850ml (1½pt) pudding basin.
2 Flake the fish, discarding any skin or bones. Mix with the breadcrumbs, parsley, lemon rind and seasoning.
3 Melt the butter for 1–1½ min and add to the fish with the beaten eggs. Mix well together.
4 Place in the greased pudding basin. Cover with clingfilm making a slit with the pointed end of a sharp knife.
5 Cook for 4–5 min, turning once halfway through.
6 Remove clingfilm and invert onto the serving dish.
7 Serve hot with tomato sauce or cold with a dressed salad.

Alternative conventional bake
Cover the pudding with greased aluminium foil or greaseproof paper and steam over a saucepan of gently boiling water for 1–1½ hrs.

100g (4oz) self-raising flour
½ × 5ml tsp (½tsp) salt
50g (2oz) shredded suet
1–2 × 5ml tsp (1–2tsp) dried
mixed herbs, optional
cold water to mix

Suet dumplings (serves 4–6)
POWER SETTING 7 (FULL OR HIGH)

1 Sift the flour and salt. Stir in the suet, herbs and sufficient cold water to form a soft manageable dough.
2 Knead lightly and form into walnut size balls, rolling between the palms of the hands with a little extra flour if necessary.
3 Drop the dumplings onto the top of a hot, simmering casserole or stew in a deep, large dish. Cover and cook until light and well risen – about 4½–5 min

– turning the dish once if necessary. Serve immediately. Alternatively, place the dumplings on a well greased plate allowing sufficient room for them to rise. Cover loosely with clingfilm making a slit with the pointed end of a sharp knife, and cook for 2–2½ min. Serve immediately with a meat casserole.

Alternative conventional bake
Place the dumplings on top of a hot, simmering casserole or stew. Cover and cook in a hot oven or on the hob for about 20 min.

Note: *These dumplings are not really suitable for freezing.*

Herbed dumplings *(serves 4–6)*
POWER SETTING 7 (FULL OR HIGH)

These are very good served with stews or casseroles instead of potatoes; almost any chopped herbs can be used to compliment the meat being served

1 Sift the flour, baking powder and salt together. Rub in the butter or margarine finely and stir in the herbs.
2 Mix in the egg and sufficient milk to make a soft but manageable dough.
3 Knead lightly and form into walnut size balls, rolling between the palms of the hands with a little extra flour if necessary.
4 Drop them onto the top of a hot simmering casserole or stew in a deep large dish. Cover and cook until light and well risen – about 4½–5 min – turning the dish once if necessary. Serve immediately. Alternatively, place the dumplings on a well greased plate, allowing sufficient room for them to rise. Cover loosely with clingfilm making a slit with the end of a sharp knife and cook for 2–2½ min. Serve immediately with a meat casserole.

100g (4oz) plain flour
1½ × 5ml tsp (1½tsp) baking powder
½ × 5ml tsp (½tsp) salt
25g (1oz) butter or margarine
3 × 15ml tbsp (3tbsp) chopped herbs, eg parsley, sage, thyme
or 3 × 5ml tsp (3tsp) dried herbs
1 egg, beaten
milk for mixing

Alternative conventional bake
Place the dumplings on top of a simmering hot casserole or stew. Cover and cook in a hot oven or on the hob for about 20 min.

Note: *These dumplings are not really suitable for freezing.*

Norfolk dumplings *(serves 4–6)*
POWER SETTING 7 (FULL OR HIGH)

These dumplings can be served with savoury meat casseroles when a few chopped herbs can be added to the mixture, or served plain with stewed fruit, jam or syrup

1 Sift the flour and salt and mix with water to form a soft but manageable dough.
2 Knead lightly and form into walnut-sized balls, rolling between the palms of the hands with a little extra flour if necessary.
3 Place in a circle on a large well greased plate allowing sufficient room for them to rise. Cover loosely with clingfilm, making a slit with the pointed end of a sharp knife.
4 Cook for 1½–2 min until light and well risen.
5 Serve immediately.

100g (4oz) self-raising flour
½ × 5ml tsp (½tsp) salt
cold water for mixing

Alternative conventional bake
Steam for 20 min in a steamer with a lid over a pan of simmering water.

Note: *These dumplings are not really suitable for freezing.*

(overleaf left) *Suet Dumplings*

(overleaf right) (front) *Cottage Pie*, (centre) *Thatched Tuna Pie*, (back) *Sausage Cobbler*

133

450g (1lb) small skinless
sausages

1 medium onion, finely
chopped

3 rashers bacon, trimmed and
cut into pieces

1 × 15ml tbsp (1tbsp) flour

2 × 5ml tsp (2tsp) soy sauce

150ml ($\frac{1}{4}$pt) milk

2 × 5ml tsp (2tsp) chopped
parsley

salt and freshly ground black
pepper

325g (11$\frac{1}{2}$oz) can sweetcorn

175g (6oz) Wholemeal Scone
Mixture (page 42)

milk for brushing

paprika pepper for sprinkling

Sausage cobbler (*serves 4*)
POWER SETTING 7 (FULL OR HIGH)

1 Place the sausages on a plate, cook for 6–7 min turning twice throughout. Drain on kitchen paper, reserving the fat, and place in a round ovenware dish.
2 Cook the onion and bacon in the fat from the sausages for 3–4 min, drain well on kitchen paper and add to the sausages.
3 Blend the flour with the soy sauce, milk, parsley, seasoning and the contents of the can of sweetcorn. Cook 5–6 min until thick, stirring every 2 min. Pour over the sausages, onions and bacon.
4 Roll out the scone dough and cut into 9–10 rounds using a 5cm (2in) cutter. Place the scone rounds over the top of the casserole, brush tops with milk and sprinkle with paprika.
5 Cook uncovered for 6–7 min until the scones are cooked and the dish is heated through.
6 Serve hot immediately.

Alternative conventional bake
When the scones are placed on the casserole, brush tops with milk and cook the dish in a preheated oven at 200°C (400°F) Mark 6 for 20–25 min.

25g (1oz) butter or margarine

1 medium onion, peeled and
chopped

2 cloves garlic, crushed or
finely chopped

100g (4oz) ham, cut into
strips

2 eggs, beaten

275ml ($\frac{1}{2}$pt) milk

100g (4oz) emmenthal or
gruyère cheese, grated

salt and freshly ground black
pepper

pinch nutmeg

450g (1lb) potatoes

25g (1oz) parmesan cheese,
grated

paprika pepper for sprinkling

Cheese and ham au gratin (*serves 4*)
POWER SETTING 7 (FULL OR HIGH) AND 4 (DEFROST OR MEDIUM)

1 Lightly grease a shallow ovenware or au gratin dish.
2 Melt the butter or margarine for 1 min in a bowl, add the onion and garlic, toss well in the fat and cook 3–4 min. Add the ham and cook for 1$\frac{1}{2}$ min.
3 Add the eggs to the milk with threequarters of the cheese, seasoning and nutmeg. Stir into the onions and ham.
4 Peel and coarsely grate the potatoes, squeeze and drain off any liquid. Add to the egg mixture. Mix well and pour into the greased dish.
5 Cover and cook on setting 4 (defrost or medium) for 18–20 min, turning every 5 min, until cooked and set.
6 Sprinkle with the remaining cheese, the parmesan cheese and paprika pepper.
7 Cook for 1–1$\frac{1}{2}$ min until the cheese is melted.
8 Serve hot with crusty french bread.

Alternative conventional bake
Cook in a preheated oven at 190°C (375°F) Mark 5 for 35–40 min. Sprinkle with the grated cheeses and return to the oven to brown the top or place under a hot grill.

Steak and kidney suet crust pie *(serves 4)*
POWER SETTING 7 (FULL OR HIGH) AND 4 (DEFROST OR MEDIUM)

An alternative to the traditional steak and kidney pudding, this dish has suet crust pastry over the top of the meat only

1 Melt the butter or margarine in a bowl for 1 min, add the onion and toss well in the butter. Cook for 2 min.
2 Trim any fat from the meat and cut into 1.25cm (½in) dice. Skin and core the kidneys, cut into small pieces and add to the meat.
3 Mix the flour and seasonings, add to the meat and toss in the flour. Add to the onion and mix well.
4 Cook for 5–6 min until the meat is browned and add the boiling stock. Stir, cover and heat until boiling for approximately 3–4 min.
5 Set the microwave to setting 4 (defrost or medium) and continue to cook the meat for a further 25–30 min.
6 Drain off most of the gravy and reserve. Place the meat into a 700–850ml (1¼–1½pt) oval pie dish and smooth the top.
7 Roll out the pastry into an oval to fit the inside of the dish. Cover the meat with the pastry and press into the side edges of the dish.
8 Cover loosely with clingfilm slit with the pointed end of a sharp knife and cook for 4½–5 min, turning once halfway through.
9 Serve hot, serving the reserved gravy separately.

Alternative conventional bake
Cover the pie loosely with greased aluminium foil and cook in a preheated oven at 200°C (400°F) Mark 6 for 25–30 min. If a brown crust is preferred, remove the foil for the last 5–10 min cooking time.

25g (1oz) butter or margarine
1 medium onion, peeled and chopped
450g (1lb) chuck steak
3 lamb's kidneys
25g (1oz) flour
salt and freshly ground black pepper
425ml (¾pt) beef stock, boiling
100g (4oz) Suet Crust Pastry (page 145)

Chicken and sweetcorn oatie pie *(serves 4)*
POWER SETTING 7 (FULL OR HIGH)

1 Lightly grease a large ovenware pie dish.
2 Blend the cornflour with a little of the stock, add the rest and cook for 1½–2 min, stirring every minute until thickened.
3 Add the chicken and the sweetcorn. Mix together, add seasoning to taste and a little extra stock if necessary to moisten. Place the mixture into the prepared pie dish.
4 Sift the flour and salt. Stir in the rolled oats and rub in the butter to form a coarse crumb mixture. Sprinkle over the chicken and sweetcorn.
5 Cook for 8–10 min until hot through and topping is cooked, giving a quarter turn every 2 min. Serve hot.

Alternative conventional bake
Cook in a preheated oven at 190°C (375°F) Mark 5 for 45–50 min.

1 × 5ml tsp (1tsp) cornflour
150ml (¼pt) chicken stock, approximately
225g (½lb) cooked chicken, roughly chopped
325g (11½oz) can sweetcorn
salt and freshly ground black pepper
100g (4oz) plain flour
pinch salt
50g (2oz) rolled oats
75g (3oz) butter or margarine

450g (1lb) potatoes, peeled
2 × 5ml tsp (2tsp) salt
boiling water
175g (6oz) cheese
1 small onion, peeled
salt and freshly ground black
pepper
25g (1oz) butter
paprika pepper for sprinkling

Cheese potato pie (serves 2–4)
POWER SETTING 7 (FULL OR HIGH)

Serve as a vegetable with a main course or on its own as a snack

1 Lightly grease an ovenware dish.
2 Slice the potatoes thinly. The slices must be very thin so use a vegetable slicer or pare with a vegetable peeler.
3 Rinse the potatoes well, place in a bowl, sprinkle with salt and just cover with boiling water. Heat in the microwave until the potatoes are transparent and soft. Drain.
4 Grate the cheese and the onion. Arrange overlapping layer of potatoes in the bottom of the prepared dish, sprinkle with salt and pepper, the grated onion, dot with butter and sprinkle with cheese. Continue the layers, alternating the potatoes with the cheese and onion, finishing with a layer of cheese.
5 Cover and cook for 6–8 min. Sprinkle with paprika and serve hot.

Alternative conventional bake
Cook covered in a preheated oven at 180°C (350°F) Mark 4 for about 20 min, remove cover and bake for another 10 min.

16 scallops, cleaned
275ml (½pt) milk
salt and freshly ground black
pepper
50g (2oz) butter
25g (1oz) flour
175g (6oz) mushrooms,
washed and sliced
150ml (¼pt) dry white wine
450g (1lb) creamed potatoes
parsley for garnish

Scallop and mushroom pie (serves 6–8)
POWER SETTING 7 (FULL OR HIGH)

This makes an excellent fish course or main course for a dinner party

1 Lightly grease a large shallow round ovenware dish.
2 Cut each scallop into 4, place with the milk and seasonings into a bowl and cook for 3–4 min. Drain and reserve the milk.
3 Melt 25g (1oz) butter for 1 min, stir in the flour until smooth. Gradually stir in the reserved milk.
4 Cook for 3–4 min until thick, stirring every minute. Beat well until smooth. Mix in scallops, mushrooms and wine.
5 Cover with piped creamed potatoes and top with slivers of the remaining butter.
6 Cook for 6–8 min or until hot through, turning every 2 min.
7 Garnish with parsley and serve hot with a side salad.

Alternative conventional bake
Cook in a preheated oven at 180°C (350°F) Mark 4 for 25–30 min.

Variation
King-size prawns may replace the scallops. Peel the prawns and add to the sauce, made from the butter, flour and milk, with the mushrooms and wine. Continue as above.

Pastry preparation: (front) *Light Wholemeal Pastry flan case ready for baking, individual pastry cases – one cooked and one uncooked, and Apple Flan ready for decoration and cooking*

450g (1lb) cod or haddock
fillet

25g (1oz) butter

½ lemon, juice and grated rind

100g (4oz) white breadcrumbs

5–6 × 15ml tbsp (5–6tbsp) oil

275ml (½pt) Tomato Sauce
(page 148)

tomato slices for garnish

Tomato fish charlotte (*serves 4*)
POWER SETTING 7 (FULL OR HIGH)

1 Lightly grease a large round dish or pie dish.
2 Skin the cod or haddock fillet, place in the greased dish, dot with the butter. Sprinkle with the lemon juice, cover and cook for 4–5 min, turning once. Drain the liquid from the fish.
3 Preheat a browning dish for 5–6 min.
4 Sprinkle the breadcrumbs with the oil, mix well to ensure they are coated with the oil.
5 Add the breadcrumbs to the preheated browning dish and cook uncovered for 1–2 min until lightly browned, stirring every ½ min. Stir in the grated lemon rind.
6 Heat the tomato sauce for 2–3 min and pour on top of the fish. Smooth the top and sprinkle on the breadcrumbs. Cook for 2–3 min until hot through.
7 Serve hot garnished with tomato slices.

Alternative conventional bake
Sauté the breadcrumbs in the oil in a heated frypan until browned. Cook the complete dish in a preheated oven at 190°C (375°F) Mark 5 for 25–30 min.

550ml (1pt) Tomato Sauce
(page 148)

225g (½lb) mushrooms,
washed and sliced

75g (3oz) wholemeal flour

75g (3oz) plain flour

½ × 5ml tsp (½tsp) salt

½ × 5ml tsp (½tsp) dry
mustard

75g (3oz) butter or margarine

75g (3oz) cheese, finely grated

tomato slices for garnish

Tomato and mushroom crumble (*serves 4–6*)
POWER SETTING 7 (FULL OR HIGH)

1 Lightly grease a large round ovenware dish.
2 Mix the tomato sauce with the sliced mushrooms and place in the greased dish.
3 Sift the flours with the salt and mustard and rub in the butter or margarine finely. Stir in the finely grated cheese.
4 Sprinkle the crumble topping lightly over the tomato mixture and smooth the top.
5 Cook for 8–10 min, giving a quarter turn every 2 min until hot through and the crumble is cooked.
6 Serve hot garnished with tomato slices.

Alternative conventional bake
Cook in a preheated oven at 190°C (375°F) Mark 5 for 40–45 min.

25g (1oz) butter or margarine

1 large onion, peeled and
finely chopped

225g (½lb) can corned beef

450g (1lb) potatoes, cooked

225g (½lb) can baked beans

salt and freshly ground black
pepper

½–1 × 5ml tsp (½–1tsp)
worcestershire sauce

paprika pepper for sprinkling,
optional

Corned beef hash (*serves 4–6*)
POWER SETTING 7 (FULL OR HIGH)

A substantial supper dish

1 Melt the butter or margarine in a large pie dish for 1 min, toss in the onion, cover and cook for 4–5 min until soft and transparent.
2 Dice the corned beef and potato. Add the corned beef and half the potato to the onion with the baked beans, seasonings and worcestershire sauce. Mix well together and smooth the top. Scatter the remaining potato over the top.
3 Cover and cook for 3–4 min until heated through.
4 Brown the potato under a hot grill or sprinkle with paprika pepper. Serve hot.

Alternative conventional bake
Cook in a preheated oven at 200°C (400°F) Mark 6 for 25–30 min until heated through and lightly browned.

Thatched tuna pie (serves 4–6)
POWER SETTING 7 (FULL OR HIGH)

1 Melt the butter or margarine in a large, round, shallow dish for 1 min, toss in the leeks, cover and cook for 3–4 min. Add the sauce and the tomatoes.
2 Drain and flake the tuna and add to the sauce with the parsley, lemon rind and juice and seasoning. Mix well together, smooth the top and clean the edges of the dish.
3 Mix the breadcrumbs with the grated cheese and sprinkle over the top of the sauce mixture. Sprinkle with a little grated nutmeg.
4 Cook for 6 min, turning every 2 min, until heated through.
5 Serve hot garnished with parsley sprigs.

Alternative conventional bake
Cook in a preheated oven at 190°C (375°F) Mark 5 for 25–30 min.

25g (1oz) butter or margarine
2 medium leeks, trimmed and finely sliced
275ml ($\frac{1}{2}$pt) Béchamel Sauce (page 147)
4 tomatoes, skinned and quartered
450g (1lb) canned tuna fish, approximately
1 × 15ml tbsp (1tbsp) chopped parsley
$\frac{1}{2}$ lemon, grated rind and juice
salt and freshly ground black pepper
50g (2oz) fresh brown breadcrumbs
50g (2oz) red leicester cheese, finely grated
grated nutmeg for sprinkling
parsley sprigs for garnish

Sausage and egg crisp (serves 4–6)
POWER SETTING 7 (FULL OR HIGH) OR 6 (ROAST OR MEDIUM/HIGH)

Simple to make but children will love this served with baked beans

1 Mix the onion with the sausagemeat, herbs and breadcrumbs.
2 Stir in the eggs and sufficient milk to form a soft mixture. Add seasonings to taste.
3 Place the mixture in a 17.5–20cm (7–8in) shallow dish. Smooth the top and cover.
4 Cook for 4 min. Allow to rest for 4 min, turn the dish and cook for a further 4–5 min. Alternatively cook on setting 6 (roast or medium/high) for 10–12 min, turning 2–3 times.
5 Drain off any fat. Crumble the potato crisps and scatter over the top of the sausagemeat.
6 Heat for 1 min and serve immediately.

Alternative conventional bake
Place in a preheated oven at 180°C (350°F) Mark 4 for 35–40 min. Add the crisp topping and cook at the same temperature for another 5 min to warm the crisps.

Note: *Do not freeze this dish with the crisp topping.*

1 medium onion, grated or finely chopped
450g (1lb) sausagemeat
1 × 15ml tbsp (1tbsp) mixed dried herbs
50g (2oz) white breadcrumbs
2 eggs, beaten
milk for mixing
salt and pepper
60–75g (2$\frac{1}{2}$–3oz) potato crisps

Miscellaneous recipes

I have included in this section basic information and recipe notes which are referred to in the various chapters throughout the book.

Pastry

The art of good pastrymaking lies in keeping the ingredients cool and handling them as little as possible. The fat is rubbed into the flour with the fingertips only (see 'Cakes' section for rubbing-in methods) and the liquid ingredients added quickly but with caution – just enough to bind the mixture together. Too much liquid will result in a sticky pastry which is difficult to roll out and which becomes hard during cooking. Roll out the pastry on a lightly floured, cool, smooth surface and avoid stretching it into shape – for example when lining a flan dish – as it will shrink back during cooking.

Not all pastries can be cooked in the microwave but the selection given here are most successful when cooked as open flan cases or as a strudel dish. Pies or tarts which use a double crust are not successful as the filling tends to cook and bubble out before the pastry is cooked.

Flans and tarts are often 'baked blind' when they are to be filled with a cold or uncooked filling. They can be made in advance, stored in the freezer and the filling added and cooked in the microwave cooker at a later date when required. The pastry quantity given in the recipes always refers to the flour weight used to make the pastry.

To line a flan dish

Roll out the pastry into a circle 5cm (2in) larger than the dish. Wrap the pastry loosely around the rolling pin and lift into the flan ring. Ease the pastry into shape removing any air from under the base, pressing well into the sides and taking care not to stretch the pastry. Cut the pastry away but leave 6mm ($\frac{1}{4}$in) above the rim of the flan dish. Carefully ease this down into the dish, or flute the edges and leave slightly higher than the rim of the dish (this allows a little extra height to the sides of the flan case to allow for any shrinkage during cooking). Alternatively roll the rolling pin across the top of the flan to cut off surplus pastry. Prick the base well with a fork.

To bake blind

Using a long, smooth strip of aluminium foil measuring approximately 3.75cm ($1\frac{1}{2}$in) wide, line the inside, upright edge of the pastry flan case. This protects the edges from overcooking in the microwave. Place two pieces of absorbent kitchen paper over the base, easing around the edges and pressing gently into the corners to help to keep the foil strip in position. Place in the microwave and cook for 4–4$\frac{1}{2}$ min on power setting 7 (full or high) giving the dish a quarter turn every minute. Remove the kitchen paper and foil and cook for a further 1–2 min.

Glacé Fruit Pudding and Lemon Foamy Sauce

Alternative conventional bake
Line the pastry flan case with a circle of lightly greased greaseproof paper (greased side down) or kitchen paper. Half fill the paper with uncooked beans, lentils, small pasta or rice which may be specially kept for this purpose. Alternatively, line the pastry flan case with foil only. Cook in a preheated oven at 200°C (400°F) Mark 6 for 15–20 min, until the pastry is nearly cooked. Remove lining and bake for 5–10 min until the base is firm and dry.

Individual pastry cases
These cases can be used to make individual flans or tarts using the fillings from various recipes in this book.

1 Roll out the pastry thinly.
2 Using inverted ramekin dishes or with tea cups as a guide, cut out circles of pastry 2.5cm (1in) larger than the rims of the inverted tea cups.
3 Place a piece of kitchen paper over the bottom of each inverted cup then shape the pastry circles over the paper and cups.
4 Arrange 4 in a circle in the microwave and cook for 4–5 min, rearranging the cups halfway through if necessary.
5 Allow to stand for 3–4 min, carefully remove pastry cases from the cups and allow to cool.

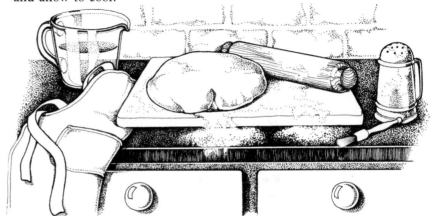

Rich shortcrust pastry

150g (6oz) plain flour
pinch salt
75g (3oz) butter
1 egg
or
1 egg yolk and 2 × 15ml tbsp (2tbsp) water

1 Sift the flour with the salt and rub in the butter finely.
2 Mix in the egg or the egg yolk beaten with the water. Knead together lightly.
3 Chill before using.

Note: *This pastry will keep well for up to 2 days in the refrigerator wrapped in clingfilm or a polythene bag.*

Sweet rich shortcrust pastry

If preferred, 2 × 5ml tsp (2tsp) caster sugar may be added to the crumb mixture before adding the egg. This gives a sweeter pastry for dishes with sweet fillings.

Light wholemeal pastry

Follow the ingredients and method for Rich Shortcrust Pastry substituting half wholemeal flour for half the plain flour.

Suet crust pastry

1 Sift the flour and salt, stir in the suet and herbs if used.
2 Mix in sufficient cold water to form a soft, manageable dough.
3 Knead lightly and use as required.

225g (½lb) self-raising flour
pinch salt
100g (4oz) shredded suet
2–3 × 5ml tsp (2–3tsp) dried mixed herbs, optional
150ml (¼pt) cold water, approximately

Almond pastry

1 Sift flour, salt and cinnamon together. Rub in the butter finely, stir in the sugar, lemon rind and ground almonds, mixing well together.
2 Beat the egg and egg yolk together and add to the dry ingredients. Mix well to form a soft dough.
3 Chill before rolling out.

225g (½lb) plain flour
pinch salt
pinch cinnamon
100g (4oz) butter
100g (4oz) caster sugar
1 lemon, grated rind
65g (2½oz) ground almonds
1 egg, beaten
1 egg yolk

Strudel paste

1 Place the flour, salt and egg in a bowl.
2 Add the oil and lemon juice. Beat vigorously until the paste leaves the sides of the bowl.
3 Cover and leave in a warm place for 30 minutes before using.

100g (4oz) plain flour
pinch salt
1 egg, beaten
1 × 15ml tbsp (1tbsp) oil
juice of 1 lemon

Sauces

The recipes given in this section are mainly a selection of sweet sauces which can be used as accompaniments to the dessert puddings. However, I have also included the basic béchamel sauce which can have other various savoury ingredients added to fill pre-cooked flan cases and pancakes before reheating in the microwave cooker.

The main advantage of cooking these sauces by microwave is that they can usually be made in their serving jugs, thereby eliminating messy pans to wash up afterwards. The sauces can be prepared and cooked in advance, then quickly reheated and taken straight to the table for serving.

Cornflour sauce (makes about 275ml [½pt])
POWER SETTING 7 (FULL OR HIGH)

1 Mix the sugar and cornflour together with a little of the milk. Gradually add the rest of the milk and the vanilla essence.
2 Cook for 3–4 min until thick, stirring every minute.

1 × 15ml tbsp (1tbsp) sugar
1 × 15ml tbsp (1tbsp) cornflour
275ml (½pt) milk
few drops vanilla essence

Brandy or sherry sauce

Omit the vanilla essence and stir in 1 × 15ml tbsp (1tbsp) brandy or sherry after cooking the sauce.

Custard sauce

Follow the ingredients and method for cornflour sauce substituting custard powder for the cornflour.

275ml (½pt) water or fruit juice
225g (½lb) marmalade
1 × 15ml tbsp (1tbsp) cornflour or arrowroot
4 × 15ml tbsp (4tbsp) cold water
lemon juice

Marmalade sauce (*makes about 425ml [¾pt]*)
POWER SETTING 7 (FULL OR HIGH)

1 Warm the water or fruit juice for 2–2½ min and stir in the marmalade.
2 Blend the cornflour or arrowroot with the cold water and stir into the marmalade. Cook for 2–3 min, stirring every minute.
3 Add lemon juice to taste.

Jam sauce

Follow the ingredients and method for Marmalade Sauce, substituting jam for the marmalade.

Syrup sauce

Follow the ingredients and method for Marmalade Sauce substituting syrup for the marmalade.

175g (6oz) plain chocolate
1 × 5ml tsp (1tsp) butter
3–4 × 15ml tbsp (3–4tbsp) golden syrup
1 × 5ml tsp (1tsp) coffee essence
150ml (¼pt) single cream

Rich chocolate sauce (*makes about 425ml [¾pt]*)
POWER SETTING 7 (FULL OR HIGH)

1 Break up the chocolate and place in a bowl with the butter, golden syrup and coffee essence.
2 Heat until melted 2–3 min, stirring once halfway through.
3 Stir in the single cream, and heat without boiling.
4 Serve hot or cold.

100g (4oz) unsalted butter
100g (4oz) caster sugar
2–3 × 15ml tbsp (2–3tbsp) rum or brandy

Rum or brandy butter (*makes about 225g [½lb]*)

Also called Hard Sauce, this is traditionally served with Christmas Pudding, but could also be served with any special hot dessert.

1 Cream the butter, add the sugar gradually, beating well together until the mixture is soft and fluffy.
2 Add the rum or brandy a little at a time, beating well after each addition.
3 Place in the serving bowl and chill in the refrigerator until hard. To make the sauce more decorative, it can be piped into the serving bowl in swirls before chilling.

Lemon foamy sauce (*makes about 275ml [½pt]*)
POWER SETTING 7 (FULL OR HIGH)

25g (1oz) butter or margarine
50g (2oz) caster sugar
1 lemon, grated rind and juice
1 egg, separated
25g (1oz) plain flour
150ml (¼pt) water

1 Cream the butter or margarine and caster sugar together until soft, beat in the lemon rind, egg yolk and flour.
2 Add the lemon juice to the water and gradually beat this into the creamed mixture. Do not worry if the mixture separates, as it will become smooth again as it cooks.
3 Heat for 2–3 min, stirring every 30 sec until thickened. If the sauce is too thick, add a little warm water and beat well.
4 Just before serving, whisk the egg white until it just holds its shape and fold into the sauce.
5 If required hot, heat slowly until warmed through by giving 15–30 sec cooking at a time.

Orange foamy sauce

Follow the ingredients and method for Lemon Foamy Sauce, substituting an orange for the lemon.

Sherry foamy sauce

Follow the ingredients and method for Lemon Foamy Sauce, substituting 2 × 15ml tbsp (2tbsp) sherry for the lemon.

Béchamel sauce (*makes about 275ml [½pt]*)
POWER SETTING 7 (FULL OR HIGH) OR 4 (DEFROST OR MEDIUM)

1 small onion
6 cloves
1 bay leaf
6 peppercorns
1 blade mace
275ml (½pt) milk
25g (1oz) butter
25g (1oz) flour
salt and pepper

This is basic white sauce but with an excellent flavour

1 Peel the onion and stick with the cloves. Place in a bowl with the rest of the spices and milk.
2 Heat without boiling. Cook for 3 min, stand for 3 min, heat for 2 min, stand for 3 min. Alternatively heat on setting 4 (defrost or medium) for 10–11 min. This allows the infusion of the flavours from the spices into the milk.
3 Melt the butter for 1 min and stir in the flour and the seasonings. Strain the milk and add a little at a time to the butter and flour mixture (called the roux), stirring continuously.
4 Cook for 1½–2 min, stirring every ½ min until thickened and bubbling. Adjust seasoning if necessary.

Quick white sauce (*makes about 275ml [½pt]*)
POWER SETTING 7 (FULL OR HIGH)

25g (1oz) butter or margarine cut into pieces
25g (1oz) flour
pinch of garlic powder
pinch dry mustard
salt and freshly ground black pepper
275ml (½pt) milk

When in a hurry, try this one-stage sauce; although it needs attention whilst cooking, it makes a good quick substitute for the Béchamel Sauce

1 Place all the ingredients into a bowl or serving jug and stir briskly or whisk. The ingredients will not combine at this stage.
2 Heat for 3–4 min, stirring or whisking every 15 sec, until cooked and thickened. As the butter or margarine melts it will absorb the flour and, providing the mixture is stirred or whisked frequently, a smooth sauce will be obtained. Adjust seasoning if necessary.

Cheese sauce

Follow the ingredients and method for either the Béchamel Sauce or the Quick White Sauce. When cooked, stir in 50–75g (2–3oz) grated cheese. Stir until melted and reheat for 30–60 sec.

1 × 15ml tbsp (1tbsp) olive oil

1 large onion, peeled and finely chopped

1–2 cloves garlic, crushed or finely chopped

400g (14oz) can tomatoes, drained

1 × 15ml tbsp (1tbsp) tomato purée

1 glass red wine or juice from tomatoes

few sprigs of fresh herbs

or

1 × 5ml tsp (1tsp) dried herbs, eg thyme or rosemary

salt and freshly ground black pepper

Tomato sauce *(makes about 275ml [½pt])*
POWER SETTING 7 (FULL OR HIGH)

1 Place olive oil, onion and garlic into a bowl and toss well. Cook for 4–5 min until soft.
2 Roughly chop the tomatoes and add to the bowl with the remaining ingredients.
3 Cook uncovered until soft and the liquid quantity is reduced giving a fairly thick sauce, stirring every 3 min.
4 Use as the basic topping for pizzas or when referred to in recipes where a good, well flavoured tomato sauce is required.

Nuts and icings

(see colour plates on pages 52 & 53)

Blanching almonds
POWER SETTING 7 (FULL OR HIGH)

Place some hot water into a bowl, bring to the boil in the microwave, add the almonds and leave to cool. Remove skins by rubbing each almond between finger and thumb. If the skins do not remove easily, reheat the almonds in the water in the microwave for 1–2 min. Rinse and dry before use.

Alternative conventional bake
Pour boiling water from a kettle over the almonds. Leave to cool and remove skins as above.

Halving almonds

Having blanched and skinned the almonds, split them in two with a sharp knife.

Shredding almonds

Having blanched, skinned and halved the almonds, cut each half into fine slivers lengthways with a sharp knife.

Flaking almonds

Having blanched and skinned the almonds, cut into thin flakes lengthways with a sharp knife.

Chopping almonds

Having blanched and skinned the almonds, chop coarsely or finely with a sharp knife.

Browning almonds
POWER SETTING 7 (FULL OR HIGH)

Place the blanched, skinned almonds onto a flat dish or plate or in a roasting bag. They may be halved, shredded, flaked or chopped. Cook in the microwave, stirring or shaking frequently until the required toasted colour. 50g (2oz) will take about 7–8 min.

Alternative conventional bake
Bake the nuts on a baking tray in a preheated oven at 180°C (350°F) Mark 4 for about 8–10 min. Alternatively, toast under a medium/hot grill, turning the almonds over when browned on one side.

Browning desiccated coconut
POWER SETTING 7 (FULL OR HIGH)

Place the coconut onto a flat dish or plate or in a roasting bag and cook in the microwave, stirring or shaking frequently, for about 5 min or until the required toasted colour.

Alternative conventional bake
Bake the coconut on a baking tray in a preheated oven at 180°C (350°F) Mark 4 for about 8–10 min. Alternatively, toast under a medium/hot grill, stirring and turning frequently.

Praline

This is not really successful in the microwave so is best made conventionally. Place equal weight quantities of unblanched almonds and caster sugar into a heavy-based saucepan and heat slowly over a low heat until the sugar is melted and turned to a nut brown colour. Stir with a metal spoon as soon as the sugar starts to colour. Turn the mixture onto an oiled tin or plate to cool. When cold, crush with a rolling pin or grind it in a blender or liquidiser. Store in an airtight container.

Apricot glaze
POWER SETTING 7 (FULL OR HIGH)

Place 450g (1lb) apricot jam in a bowl with 2 × 15ml tbsp (2tbsp) lemon juice and 4 × 15ml tbsp (4tbsp) water. Mix well together and then bring to the boil in the microwave. Allow to boil for 2–3 min, stirring frequently. Sieve and allow to cool and thicken slightly before use. This keeps very well in a covered jar so can be made in large quantities.

Soft icing

Mix together 3 × 15ml tbsp (3tbsp) sifted icing sugar and 1–2 × 15ml tbsp (1–2tbsp) golden syrup. Beat well together adding a little more icing sugar or golden syrup until a soft consistency is obtained.

Note: *Do not freeze this icing.*

Glacé icing

Mix 175g (6oz) sifted icing sugar with sufficient hot water to make a soft paste, thick enough to coat the back of the spoon. Mix well and use immediately.

Note: *Do not freeze this icing.*

Feathered icing

Make up Glacé Icing and coat the top of the cake. With a fine paintbrush, draw lines with two food colourings alternately across the surface of the icing or in graduated circles from the centre to the outside edge. Alternatively, pipe tinted glacé icing in lines using a fine writing nozzle. Draw a fine skewer through the lines of colouring, alternating the direction to give a feathered effect. Leave to set before cutting the cake.

Note: *Do not freeze this icing.*

Ginger glacé icing

Sift 175g (6oz) icing sugar together with 1 × 5ml tsp (1tsp) ground ginger. Mix with sufficient hot water to make a soft paste, thick enough to coat the back of a spoon. Mix well and use immediately.

Note: *Do not freeze this icing.*

Orange or lemon glacé icing

Mix together 175g (6oz) sifted icing sugar with sufficient strained orange or lemon juice to give a thick icing. A few drops of orange or lemon colouring may be added to give a little more colour.

Note: *Do not freeze this icing.*

Coffee or chocolate glacé icing

Sift 175g (6oz) icing sugar into a bowl. Dissolve a little instant coffee or cocoa powder in hot water and add to the icing sugar to make a soft paste, thick enough to coat the back of a spoon.

Note: *Do not freeze this icing.*

Buttercream 1

Soften 75g (3oz) butter and gradually add 175g (6oz) sifted icing sugar. Beat well after each addition and then beat until light and fluffy. Flavour and colour as required.

Buttercream 2

Whisk 2 egg whites and 100g (4oz) sifted icing sugar together over a bowl of hot water until thick and the mixture holds its shape. Cream 225g (8oz) unsalted butter until soft, then gradually add the egg white and icing sugar mixture. Flavour and colour as required.

Buttercream flavourings

Chocolate: Melted plain chocolate or a little cocoa powder dissolved in warm water.
Coffee: Coffee essence or a little instant coffee dissolved in warm water.
Orange: Finely grated rind of orange.
Lemon: Finely grated rind of lemon.

Quick American frosting

2 egg whites
400g (14oz) caster sugar
pinch salt
4 × 15ml tbsp (4tbsp) water
2 × 5ml tsp (2tsp) cream of tartar

1 If using an electric table mixer, place all ingredients except the cream of tartar into the bowl and whisk on full speed for 15 sec. When stiff add the cream of tartar.
2 If using a hand mixer or rotary whisk, place all ingredients into a bowl over a bowl or pan of hot water and whisk for 5 min. Remove from the heat and allow to cool for 4–5 min. Whisk again until thick and shiny and holding shape.
3 This quantity is sufficient to coat the outside of a 20–22.5cm (8–9in) cake. Half quantity would be sufficient to coat the outside of a 15–17.5cm (6–7in) cake.

Note: *This frosting is best eaten on the day it is made and is not suitable for freezing.*

151

25g (1oz) butter

50g (2oz) soft brown or demerara sugar

2 × 15ml tbsp (2tbsp) cocoa

3 × 15ml tbsp (3tbsp) cold water

2 × 5ml tsp (2tsp) milk

225g (½lb) icing sugar, sifted

2 × 15ml tbsp (2tbsp) warm water

few drops vanilla essence

Chocolate fudge icing
POWER SETTING 7 (FULL OR HIGH)

1 Place the butter and sugar into a large bowl. Blend the cocoa with the cold water and add to the bowl with the milk.
2 Heat for 1–2 min, stir until the sugar is dissolved.
3 Heat until boiling, then allow to boil for 2–2½ min.
4 Add icing sugar, warm water and vanilla essence. Mix well together then beat well for 5 min.
5 Pour over the cake whilst still warm as this icing sets when cold.

Chocolate caraque
POWER SETTING 7 (FULL OR HIGH)

Melt about 75g (3oz) plain chocolate for 2–3 min. Stir until smooth and spread the chocolate thinly onto a flat, smooth surface such as a work top, marble slab or laminate chopping board. When nearly set, using a long, sharp knife and a slight sawing movement, shave the chocolate off the top surface holding the knife almost upright. Long rolls or flakes will form which are best chilled in the refrigerator before using to decorate a cake.

Acknowledgements

I should like to thank Trish Davies, Angela Voller and Jane Fletcher for their help in testing the recipes and Kate Norman for her assistance in preparing the food for photography. To Thorn Domestic Appliances (Electrical) Limited I offer my grateful thanks for supplying Tricity and Moffat microwave cookers and assisting with the photography. Colour photography by John Plimmer, RPM Photographic, Havant. Line illustrations by Evelyn Bartlett.

Index